Becoming an

ASA

Assistant

Books are to be returned on or before
the last date below.

Also available from A & C Black:

Swimming Games and Activities
Second Edition
Jim Noble and Alan Cregeen

Swimming for Fitness
Second Edition
George Austin and Jim Noble

Know The Game Swimming
Second Edition
Amateur Swimming Association

Becoming an
ASA
Assistant
Teacher

A GUIDE

Phil Butler

A & C Black • London

Dedicated to Frances

Published in 2000 by A & C Black (Publishers) Ltd
35 Bedford Row, London WC1R 4JH

Previously published by Phil Butler as *A Guide to Becoming an ASA Assistant Teacher* (1997)

ISBN 0 7136 5349 3

A CIP catalogue record for this book is available from the British Library.

Acknowledgement
Illustrations by Steve Bayley

Note: Whilst every effort has been made to ensure that the content of this book is as technically accurate and as sound as possible, neither the authors nor the publishers can accept responsibility for any injury or loss sustained as a result of the use of this material.

Typeset in 13/13pt Perpetua

Printed and bound in Great Britain by Martins the Printers, Berwick upon Tweed

Contents

Additional Skills

Chapter 11 Survival Skills 117

Chapter 12 The Club Swimmer and Environment 136

Acknowledgements

Steve Bayley – incredible dedication to the cause of producing the drawings I had in mind, with great humour.

Nick Barber – vast amount of computer scanning of Steve's drawings.

Rick Johnstone – being 'the spark' especially in my early tutoring career, and the unenviable task of proofreading.

Sylvia Owens – Proofreading from a non-specialist viewpoint.

Jack Goodwin – providing the impetus for getting me involved in swimming teaching.

Mum – for everything!

David Bradbury – for giving me my chance in full-time swimming education.

Becky – patience, tolerance and encouragement as I cursed the computer and burnt the midnight oil.

The Amateur Swimming Association for allowing the reproduction of documentation applicable to the course.

Terminology

The following terms are used throughout the book, and the definitions below provide a general guide to their meaning:

Teacher A person generally dealing with stroke and skill improvement in a non-lane setting.

Coach A person generally dealing with more able swimmers in a lane setting whether focusing on technique, stamina and speed or other physiological aspects.

Lesson Usually no more than thirty minutes and focusing mainly on technique, run by a teacher in a non-lane setting.

Session Usually more than thirty minutes and focusing on technique or physiological aspects, run by a coach in a lane setting.

Note: Throughout the book individuals are referred to as 'he'. This is purely for ease of reference and should, of course, be taken to mean 'he or she' where appropriate.

Foreword

Phil has twelve years of tutoring experience, during which time he has tutored over 150 courses at a number of different centres in the Midlands and north-west of England.

A full-time professional swimming teacher, Phil has also participated in Masters swimming and life saving competitions (having run his own Life Saving club for fourteen years).

This book is a product of Phil's considered opinion and tried-and-tested experiences, as well as his in-depth knowledge and awareness of the needs and requirements of trainee swimming teachers. Covering all the requirements of the ASA Assistant Teacher syllabus, this manual will be a welcome addition to the reference material available to the aspiring teacher, and also an interesting and informative resource for those already qualified.

EM Johnstone
Former ASA Principal Tutor

Introduction

Thank you for deciding to purchase this book. I hope your decision is an indication that you have already started, or are about to embark on, an ASA Assistant Teacher course.

This book has been designed, as the title would suggest, as a complete guide to all the different aspects of the ASA Assistant Teacher course. The content is linked to the syllabus laid out in the ASA Teaching and Coaching regulations and you should receive a copy of these regulations at the beginning of the course. Normally, every endeavour is made to furnish you with a copy as soon as you have fully enrolled in a course. You should refer to the pages which specifically relate to the course on a regular basis and in addition read the general regulations. You will also receive a log book at the beginning of the course, and guidance is offered here to assist you in completing it.

The book is structured to cover the syllabus of an ASA Assistant Teacher course in a logical manner; however, some chapters are interdependent and it may be necessary to read them out of their current order.

I have written this guide in an easy-to-read style and with a 'splash' of humour. I'm sure you'll find the superb illustrations stimulating. Steve Bayley was able to depict my ideas accurately, however strange they seemed. I will remain forever indebted to him.

Throughout this book the circled numbers that appear as part of an illustration refer to the corresponding point in the relevant section of text. For example, ① in the illustration Fig. 7.1 on page 56 refers to point (1) in the section, Front Crawl – Body position.

Please remember that the Assistant Teacher course is the entry level to the ASA Teaching and Coaching qualifications, so the course tutor will be sympathetic to the fact that you may as yet have little or no knowledge about swimming. (You soon will have though!) Everything possible will be done to help you achieve the assessment criteria; listen and act upon the advice offered to you by the course tutor and moderator; read this book and any other information given to you by the course tutor.

I sincerely hope that you enjoy reading this book.

Good luck!

The ASA

Assistant

Teacher

Chapter 1
About the ASA Assistant Teacher Course

Assessment Criteria

During an ASA Assistant Teacher course you will be working towards achieving certain criteria. The assessment criteria for 1999/2000 are displayed in Table 1.1 (*see* pages 2–3). These criteria are subject to review each year. Both the course tutor and the course moderator will refer to them during the course and will mark them with you at the end. While at first sight the criteria may appear a little daunting, they are readily achievable if you follow the advice given to you by the course tutor and moderator.

Observation Assessment Sheet for the ASA Assistant Teacher Certificate Swimming.   AS2/AT

Candidate's Name:.................................... Date: .... Venue:..................................

Course Tutor (assessor) .... Course Moderator (internal verifier)...........................

Important note to candidates: This Observation Assessment Sheet is your summative assessment for the practical aspect of the course. Every ✓ in the yes column indicates where the appropriate standard has been reached. Any ✓ in the No column indicates areas which require further development. These aspects should form the basis of your Individual Action Plan

- *Denotes changes from 01.09.96*

Has the candidate:

1.	• Log Book	Y	N
• i	completed the personal details?		
• ii	completed plans for personal development?		
iii	demonstrated simple planning methods?		
iv	demonstrated simple record keeping methods?		
Comments:			

2.	Conducting the Sessions	Y	N
• i	organised the facility and equipment efficiently?		
ii	dressed appropriately for the sessions?		
iii	outlined the objectives for the sessions?		
iv	utilised appropriate swimming aids?		
v	developed the sessions progressively?		
vi	demonstrated effective use of a variety of teaching methods?		
• vii	implemented the session plan to suit the needs of the group?		
viii	shown an ability to respond to the needs of the individual?		
ix	established and maintained control of the groups?		
x	checked the number of participants at the end of the sessions?		
xi	assisted with the orderly departure of the participants?		
xii	made effective use of the time available?		
xiii	made effective use of the space available?		
Comments			

Table 1.1 *Observation Assessment Sheet for the ASA Assistant Teacher Certificate Swimming 1999/2000*

3.	Communication	Y	N
i	demonstrated effective positioning on the poolside?		
ii	demonstrated effective positioning in the water?		
iii	given praise when appropriate?		
iv	provided feedback on performance in a positive manner?		
• v	given clear and accurate verbal explanations?		
• vi	given clear and accurate visual demonstrations?		
vii	established and maintained relationship with participants?		
viii	motivated the participants?		

Comments

4.	Technical Knowledge	Y	N
i	demonstrated an understanding of the basic fundamentals of swimming?		
ii	demonstrated an understanding of the needs of the non swimmer?		
iii	demonstrated a basic understanding of the four competitive strokes?		
iv	demonstrated an understanding of a range of aquatic skills?		
vi	demonstrated an understanding of the basic principles of skill analysis?		
• vii	demonstrated a basic understanding of the needs of early competition swimmers?		
viii	demonstrated an understanding of the basic principles of work and rest?		

Comments:

5.	Safety	Y	N
i	outlined rules and safety issues?		
ii	maintained a safe teaching environment?		

Comments:

Candidates Name: ....

Signed: ....candidate   ....tutor (assessor)   ....moderator(internal verifier)

NOTE: *Permission has been granted by the Amateur Swimming Association for this assessment form to be used in connection with the publication* Becoming an ASA Assistant Teacher: A Guide. *The assessment decisions made as part of the process of working through the publication does not indicate that the ASA has been involved in, or has agreed or disagreed with, any assessment decision made. The only assessment decisions attributable to the ASA are those arrived at as a result of a registered ASA course.*

A Guide to the Assessment Criteria

Each of the criteria contained in Table 1.1 is explained in detail to guide you on what is required. The numbering, headings and the order correspond to Table 1.1 for easy reference.

1 Log book

i *Completed the personal details?*
Give as much information as possible.

ii *Completed plans for personal development?*
Be as realistic as possible. Detail how you will achieve your goals, i.e. attending courses, helping other teachers at other venues, reading certain relevant publications.

iii *Demonstrated simple planning methods?*
Include a copy of any lesson plans which have been written for you on the course. Obtain a lesson plan from any other teacher who you assisted outside of the course (you may have to plead a little). Include all lesson plans that you have written yourself.

iv *Demonstrated simple record keeping methods?*
Complete an evaluation for every lesson you teach as soon as possible after the lesson. Record times of swimmers during the training schedules. Record as much information as possible while carrying out any analysis. Don't forget the simple things: date, name of swimmer, stroke or skill, etc.

2 Conducting the sessions

i *Organised the facility and equipment efficiently?*
Is the required equipment at the teaching station before you are due to teach? Is it stored in a safe manner?

ii *Dressed appropriately for the sessions?*
Do you look professional? Is your dress non-restrictive?

iii *Outlined the objectives for the sessions?*
Do the swimmers know what they are going to do and why, at the beginning of the lesson?

iv *Utilised appropriate swimming aids?*
Are you using aids appropriate to the group you are working with: i.e. toys, arm-discs and rubber rings as necessary with non-swimmers; pull-buoys only with advanced or club swimmers, and so on?

v *Developed the sessions progressively?*
Are you using the whole/part/whole method? Are the part practices that you use during the lesson becoming more difficult? Generally, do your teaching points start in a basic manner and become more detailed as the lesson progresses?

vi *Demonstrated effective use of a variety of teaching methods?*
Do you include the use of pupil demonstrations to apply peer pressure? Are you asking the children questions to actively include them in their own learning?

vii *Implemented the session plan to suit the needs of the group?*
Do you amend the plan if it is pitched either too low or too high? Do you tailor particular practices to suit individuals who may be progressing either more slowly or quickly than others?

viii *Shown an ability to respond to the needs of the individual?*
In addition to **vii** above, do you encourage an individual who is perhaps less confident or more timid? Do you channel the energies of an individual who is possibly dominating or demanding too much attention?

ix *Established and maintained control of the groups?*

Do you establish clear behavioural expectations at the beginning of the lesson? Do you encourage and reward good behaviour? Do you chastise poorly behaved children in an appropriate manner?

x *Checked the number of participants at the end of the sessions?*

Do you check the number of participants in each session – not only at the end, but also throughout the lesson, especially when children have asked to visit the toilet?

xi *Assisted with the orderly departure of the participants?*

Do you ensure that the children return safely to the appropriate changing room?

xii *Made effective use of the time available?*

Are the children active for most of the time? Is your talking kept to the minimum between practices? Are you totally involved throughout the whole lesson?

xiii *Made effective use of the space available?*

Do the children have sufficient space in which to perform any activity in complete safety? Do you encourage them to perform in a different manner other than widths if appropriate, i.e. circuits, at the rail, or across the area?

3 Communication

i *Demonstrated effective positioning on the poolside?*

Are you always in a position where you can see, and be seen by, everyone at all times? Do you stand well back when performing your demonstrations? Do you use the end of the pool, whenever you are using a teaching station which is situated at the end of the pool?

ii *Demonstrated effective positioning in the water?*

Are you in a position where you can see all the children in your charge? Do you keep a distance to discourage the children from becoming over-familiar? Do you keep a low position in the water when necessary, in order to be reassuring?

iii *Given praise when appropriate?*

Do you recognise and reward effort, improvement and good behaviour?

iv *Provided feedback on performance in a positive manner?*

Do you comment on the point you have just asked them to concentrate on? Do you give information on how to further improve, without using the word 'don't'?

v *Given clear and accurate verbal explanations?*

Do you use language appropriate to the group you are working with? Do you check to see that they understand your instructions and your teaching points?

vi *Given clear and accurate visual demonstrations?*

Do you adopt a position which puts you in the correct plane? Do you stand back when demonstrating? Do you perform an accurate rendition of the strokes and skills? Are your pupil demonstrations given by the most able in your group, or by a swimmer from a more advanced group? Are the other swimmers in a good position (normally on the poolside) to observe a pupil demonstration?

vii *Established and maintained relationship with participants?*

Are the swimmers relaxed and responding well? Do children show an appropriate amount of respect? Are you in control?

viii *Motivated the participants?*
Are the swimmers eager to please? Are they looking for information from you with regard to their performance? Do they listen intently to you? Are they attempting to impress you in order to become a demonstrator?

4 Technical knowledge
i *Demonstrated an understanding of the basic fundamentals of swimming?*
Are you adapting the appropriate body positions for differing body types? Are you encouraging the correct hand shape? Are non-swimmers being encouraged to keep movements beneath the surface of the water? Are you teaching bent-arm pulls, etc. where appropriate?

ii *Demonstrated an understanding of the needs of the non-swimmer?*
Are you teaching propulsive movements and underwater recovery? Are you empathetic to the potential worries of non-swimmers? Are you positive and encouraging and continually offering advice?

iii *Demonstrated a basic understanding of the four competitive strokes?*
Are you working on the aspects of strokes most relevant to the group you are with – for example, body position and leg action with children who are only just able to swim? Do you give correct information on the strokes? Do you give a variety of teaching points in relation to the aspect of the stroke you are working on?

iv *Demonstrated an understanding of a range of aquatic skills?*
Are you *teaching* rather than just allowing for the practice of survival skills? Are you working on the correct aspect of those skills?

For an unknown reason there is no criterion v number.

vi *Demonstrated an understanding of the basic principles of skill analysis?*
Do you analyse in the order of '**blabt**' (**b**ody position, **l**eg action, **a**rm action, **b**reathing technique, **t**iming or co-ordination)? Do you record good points of technique, as well as poor? When delivering the results of your analysis to a swimmer, do you 'sandwich' the information (i.e. give positive feedback followed by negative, and ending on a positive note)?

vii *Demonstrated a basic understanding of the needs of early competition swimmers ?*
Do you help to educate them in the use of the clock? Do you give help in calculations as needed? Do you motivate them throughout, explaining why they are doing a particular piece of work?

viii *Demonstrated an understanding of the basic principles of work and rest?*
Are you giving adequate periods of rest in order for performance levels to continue – yet not giving too much rest so that any training effect is lost?

5 Safety
i *Outlined rules and safety issues?*
Do you check that they know the emergency procedure? Do you briefly go through safety issues, such as no running, etc.?

ii *Maintained a safe teaching environment?*
Do the children in your control understand the emergency procedure? Do they behave in a safe manner and consider the other participants? Do they understand that they should do nothing except on your command? Do they enter the water safely? Do you ensure that hair is tied back, jewellery is removed and that no-one is chewing?

Teaching and Coaching Analysis

During the course, you are required in accordance with the ASA regulations to carry out analyses of other teachers and coaches. This is aimed at making you more aware of good teaching techniques, other methods of presentation and ways to achieve your goal.

The questions are designed to act as prompts to help you to carry out an analysis with greater ease. It is advisable to do a written analysis. It is important to remember to remain as unobtrusive as possible while watching other teachers. You should not distract either the swimmers or the teacher. If a teacher is doing a 'good job' you will often have little need to hear them. You will be able to discern exactly what is happening just by watching.

Answer the following questions:

- Is the teacher of a pleasant disposition?
- Are they stimulating the swimmers?
- Are the swimmers attentive to them?
- Do they control the group?
- Is the teacher vigilant at all times?
- Do they provide accurate teacher demonstrations?
- Do they provide pupil demonstrations?
- Are they working at the correct level?
- Any other observations not covered by the above?
- Any ideas that you may 'steal'?

Use the space below to write a brief summary of what you have observed.

Stroke Analysis

You will also be required by ASA regulations to carry out stroke and skills analyses. The chart below provides an example of the kind of format you could use. (*See* page 9 for guidelines on actually carrying out a stroke analysis.)

Before you are able to accurately carry out a stroke analysis, you must of course have a reasonable idea of what the stroke should look like and what you need to observe. It is therefore advisable to read The Strokes section before attempting this task.

Be patient, as the skill of performing an analysis takes a while to acquire.

SWIMMER'S NAME	STROKE	DATE	TEACHER
Further information			
First general impression			
Body position			
Leg action			
Arm action			
Breathing			
Timing (co-ordination)			
Action required and other comments			

Table 1.2 *Stroke and Skill Analysis*

Guide to Table 1.2

Your tutor should guide you through the task of stroke/skill analysis.

NAME/STROKE/DATE/TEACHER

This section is important, since the analysis may be part of an ongoing monitoring of this swimmer. Different teachers may have differing opinions.

FURTHER INFORMATION

- Was the analysis done under 'normal' conditions, at the end of a session, or at the beginning?
- Did the swimmer show signs of illness?

FIRST GENERAL IMPRESSION

- Does the swimmer look relaxed, able to prolong this level of performance, able to go faster, proficient, and so on?

BODY POSITION

- Be logical: start at the head and work down the body.
- Ignore, at this stage, movements of the arms and legs.
- Consider only the position of the legs in relation to the body.
- Is the swimmer in a streamlined position?
- Is the body still?
- Remember to record good points. Refer to your 'model' of the stroke.

LEG ACTION

- Does the leg-kick look efficient? If appropriate to the stroke, try to break the kick down further into two sections: *propulsive* and *recovery*.
- First look for obvious points relevant to the stroke – i.e. are the toes pointed, are the feet turned out and kicking at the same time as each other.
- Then, look in detail – i.e. are the feet 'intoed'? Any variations?

ARM ACTION

- Does the arm action look efficient?
- Break down the arm action into at least propulsive and recovery phases.
- Where possible, break down further into *entry*, *propulsive* and *recovery*. Remember to look for sweeping movements.
- First look for the obvious (i.e. fingers together), and then for detail (i.e. length and pathway of pull).

BREATHING

- Is there evidence of aquatic breathing, or are they holding their breath?
- Do they have a regular pattern?
- Do they look comfortable in breathing or does it appear to hinder their ability to continue to perform the stroke for any prolonged period of time?

TIMING (CO-ORDINATION)

- How are the legs timed to the arms? For example, is the swimmer using a six-beat leg-kick in Front Crawl.
- How is the breathing timed to the arm action?
- How are the arms timed to one another, if relevant?
- This area is the most difficult to observe. Please ask your tutor or coach if you are having problems when on the poolside.

ACTION REQUIRED AND OTHER COMMENTS

- What would be the most beneficial aspect of the stroke to work on in order to create the best effect?
- Are there any irregularities which you would not normally observe?

Please note that analysis requires a great deal of practice – so do practise!

Chapter 2
The Teacher/Coach

Qualities of a Swimming Teacher

As a teacher of swimming, just as in any other subject, you will need a wide range of qualities to enable you to deal with all circumstances. As you gain experience they will undoubtedly develop. The following list contains the essential qualities needed, but is not an exhaustive one. Most of these qualities will be required in order for you to meet the criteria of the ASA Assistant Teacher Certificate Swimming (these are detailed on pages 2–6).

Fig. 2.1 *Communication*

1 Communicator

- The essence of any good teacher is the ability to communicate.
- You will use mainly visual and verbal methods of communication.
- You will need to be able to communicate verbally at many different levels, from 3- to 83 year olds, in an audible and stimulating manner.

2 Knowledge of the subject

- To gain respect from students, parents and other teachers it is essential to 'know your stuff'. Swimmers will soon know if you don't.

Fig. 2.2 *Knowledge*

Fig. 2.3 *Patience*

- You will need to continually update and increase your knowledge. Cover all areas but concentrate on your weaker ones.
- Always be prepared to admit to not knowing an answer, but make sure you always find out for the next session.

3 Patience

You will undoubtedly encounter a number of different types of students who will 'test' you for a variety of reasons.

- The reluctant, timid learner who may have an exaggerated fear.
- The over-exuberant swimmer, whose energies may need channelling.
- The 'trier' who is taking longer than others to acquire the skill.
- The over-enthusiastic parent.

4 Empathy

You must empathise with different individuals for a variety of reasons.

- The pupil who is scared may have a justifiable reason for their fear.
- The child who is very exuberant may be experiencing their only treat or chance to expend their energy.

Fig. 2.4 *Empathy*

- The adult learner who may be filled with embarrassment.
- The child who is always the slowest may still be trying just as hard as all the other pupils.

5 Management and controlling skills

- Swimmers – and particularly younger children – may have little idea of the behaviour expected from them; they will need to be educated in order to create a safe environment which is conducive to learning.
- You will need to manage both space and time to ensure that all possible activity is performed in safety.

Fig. 2.5 *Management*

Fig. 2.6 *Enthusiasm*

- You will have to firmly show 'who is the boss', in a pleasant manner.

6 Enthusiasm

- Children will show a great desire both to learn and to please you. However, this must be met by you with equal – and possibly more – of a wish to help educate them in the manner in which you would wish to be educated by another teacher.
- If you display little enthusiasm towards swimmers, then they will soon sense this and they will quickly lose interest and cause problems for you.

7 Motivator

Different individuals will respond to differing forms of motivation.

Fig. 2.7 *Motivator*

- Some will readily accept a challenge, while others may respond negatively.
- Younger swimmers in particular may be motivated by reward – for example, an ASA award, a team point or a star from a class teacher.
- Most children will be motivated if there is the chance to be the class demonstrator or the opportunity to progress into another group.
- Some children may simply want to please you, and themselves.

It is your job to find out which individuals respond to which form of motivation.

Communication

Definition The imparting or exchange of information, ideas or feelings.

There are three types of communication we are likely to use when teaching swimming:

- Verbal
- Visual
- Manual

Verbal

It would be very difficult to conduct a swimming lesson without speech, but there are many areas to be considered to ensure that verbal communication is as effective as it should be.

1 Comprehension
How much of everyday adult language do children understand?

Consider the following words, and ask yourself if an eight-year-old child would understand them: *technique, extended, flexible, pike, accelerate, vertical, horizontal, streamlined.* Although they are words which you might normally use when teaching certain aquatic

Fig. 2.8 *Verbal communication*

skills, it is unlikely that the average eight-year-old would understand you. In fact, some older children might struggle to understand you if you were using this kind of vocabulary.

A more successful way of expressing such words might be: technique – *the way you do it*; extended – *stretched*; flexible – *floppy or loose*; pike – *bend at your tummy*; accelerate – *speed up or go faster*; vertical – *upright or standing position*; horizontal – *lying position*; streamlined – *neat and narrow.*

Of course, you must ensure that you do not talk 'down' to the children. You could use the more technical words but check first that the children understand what you are trying to say. All teaching points should contain language which is appropriate to that particular class, irrespective of age. Remember also that a visual accompaniment to any teaching point is vital for clear comprehension in the learning of physical skills.

You can help further by using stimulating and highly descriptive teaching points. One way of doing this is to attempt to 'paint a picture with words', since children learn by imitation and imagery to a high degree. So 'stretched' could become stretched like:

Fig. 2.9 *Stretched like Superman*

Fig. 2.10 *Stretched like a crocodile*

- Superman
- a crocodile
- a spear
- a giant.

The child is far more likely to remember and think about what you are asking if it is appealing to them.

In an article by Joan Ingram entitled 'Swimming Should Be Fun', which appeared in *Swimming Times* (July 1989), children were asked for their descriptions of certain shapes as they related to aquatic skills. When shown a mushroom float, their various responses were as follows: iceberg, ball, tortoise, buoy, jellyfish, balloon, orange, shell. The name 'mushroom float' is curious, since it relates neither to floating, nor to water. Imagine, from an eight-year-old's point of view, how much more fun it would be to pretend to be a jellyfish…rather than a mushroom!

If you want to increase your repertoire of ideas in order to relate more to children, you can help yourself by exploring current fads – for example, Teenage Ninja Turtles, Transformers, Tazos, Spice Girls, Boyzone, Antz – and then by trying to adapt a few teaching points to include them.

Fig. 2.12 *Float like a mushroom*

Fig. 2.11 *Float like a jellyfish*

Fig. 2.13 *Delivery*

2 Delivery

Since a swimming pool is a very noisy environment, it is sometimes difficult to make yourself heard. Therefore, try the following techniques.

- Say as little as possible to communicate the point of technique you are working on. There is less chance of being misunderstood. 'Lift your elbow' may be sufficient.

- Control your environment so that the need for excessive volume is minimised. In other words, make sure all pupils are quiet while you speak (four children splashing in the water while you are talking is quite noisy); ask other teachers to moderate their volume if they are being excessively loud.

- Project your voice, but avoid shouting. You will need to practise this, but you will not enjoy teaching if you have to shout. Also, you are more likely to lose control.

- Speak with good inflexion and intonation. A monotone drone soon becomes boring and you will lose the attention of your pupils.

- Any verbal communication should usually be positive. Avoid 'don'ts', as you will be continually re-enforcing negative points rather than the correct points of technique. Pupils need to hear what *to do*, not what *not to do* – i.e., 'turn your head to breathe' rather than, 'don't lift your head to breathe'.

Visual

The value of visual communication cannot be too highly stressed. It can account for up to 80 per cent of the learning of a physical skill. Since swimming is a physical skill, pupils should be given many opportunities to see the skill before attempting to copy it.

Can you imagine trying to teach a pupil the skill of kicking or throwing a ball, but without being able to show them first? Worse still, imagine what it would be like for the pupil if the skill is only described to them, with no image to help them.

Visual communication is an essential tool in your 'armoury'; it will ensure that your teaching is effective as well as optimising the pupil's chance of success.

1 Demonstration

Now that you are aware of the importance of demonstrations, you must also be very conscious of the accuracy of any demonstration provided – whether by the teacher or by another pupil. Children especially are excellent imitators and are likely to copy exactly what they see. (You may experience this first hand, when working with three- to five-year-olds. For

Fig. 2.15 *Demonstration (b)*

example, you provide a teacher demonstration of a Front Crawl leg-kick by using your arms as the legs performing the kick. The children then proceed to swim, 'waggling' their arms just as you showed them!) Teacher demonstrations should be given continuously, accompanying where possible each teaching practice and point.

It may be necessary to give a demonstration of both the practice *and* the point, i.e. showing how to hold the float (the practice) *and* showing a turned foot (the point).

It is also desirable, whenever possible, to communicate with the pupils *as they are*

Fig. 2.14 *Demonstration (a)*

Fig. 2.16 *Demonstration (c)*

Fig. 2.17 *Demonstrate the practice and the point*

Fig. 2.18 *Pupil demonstrations*

actually performing the skill. This is the optimum time for them to acquire and remember it. Visual communication is most likely to enable this, since the pupils may not be able to hear you.

Pupil demonstrations should be used throughout the lesson, but more sporadically than teacher demonstrations. This is because time can be lost by the pupils climbing out of the pool for a good vantage point. Remember that it is also advantageous for pupils to see part-practices being performed as well as whole strokes or skills. Pupil demonstrations also provide an excellent method of providing peer pressure in a lesson, but be careful not to create a situation where you have either prima donnas or failures.

Generally, the value of pupil demonstrations is higher than that of teacher demonstrations because the skill is being performed in its natural environment with the correct forces being experienced and the swimmer in the most natural position. After any pupil demonstration, remember to give the other pupils the chance to copy.

Fig. 2.19 *Positioning*

2 Positioning

Whenever you are teaching swimming, it is imperative that you can always be seen by every pupil in order that they may see your demonstrations. It is even more important that you can see them, for safety reasons, and so that you are able to observe their performance. It will be necessary for you to move around to ensure that you are in the correct position. You should however minimise this so that you don't become too warm, and also because the children need to know where you are. However, avoid encroaching into the pupils' personal space; no-one likes it, and you will also increase the chance of any demonstration that you do being seen incorrectly.

3 Body language

The manner in which you present yourself will influence your pupils' reaction to you. If you appear confident and in control you are far more likely to gain their respect. On the other hand, if you are timid, restrictive and defensive with your body signals, then your pupils will sense it.

Your facial expression will help dramatically in this respect. It is important that you smile, because if the pupils sense that you are enjoying yourself and that you

are approachable, then they are far more likely to enjoy themselves. Encourage them with your facial expression and ensure you have eye contact with all pupils as much as possible; they will then feel a part of the lesson, irrespective of their ability, and are far more likely to pay attention to you.

It is possible to slip into the habit of being aggressive and intimidating in your gestures. Can you remember any of your teachers with arms folded or hands on hips, glaring at you? Such gestures may on odd occasions be used to your advantage if a child is being particularly disruptive, even after gentle warnings. If you do have to resort to this tactic then it is important to explore possible explanations as to why it is necessary. Are the pupils bored or inactive?

A good teacher usually has some of the characteristics of a good actor, since a variety of presentations will be required depending on who is being taught. Practise being firm, fun, lively, calm, authoritarian, encouraging and motivational.

Your appearance can also be a good method of communicating with and stimulating children. In the past, swimming 'instructors' wore only conventional

Fig. 2.20 *Avoid aggressive body language*

clothing. While this was functional, it was also a little boring and did little to stimulate children. Children, especially the very young, relate to bright colours and vivid patterns which are readily available in the sports clothes market. Such clothing can therefore be a useful medium to help children relate to you, although it is important that you never wear anything which could be deemed offensive in any way or in which you do not feel comfortable.

4 Visual communication from other sources

At certain pools you may have access to a chalkboard, or whiteboard. Use these fully to explain – probably diagrammatically – any skills that pupils are struggling to comprehend. Remember to be both brief and accurate. You may also communicate instructions of schedules, awards, and so on. Charts of numerous skills are available and are invaluable in helping to provide pictorial images of difficult skills. Again, remember to be brief.

With more able pupils (probably club swimmer standard or similar), it can be useful to film them to analyse their skills more thoroughly. You can then provide excellent feedback at your leisure, using freeze frame, without wasting very valuable pool time. You may also be able to communicate with this level of swimmer through instructional videos and personal computer programmes.

Verbal and Visual Feedback

One of the most important features of any good teaching performance is to provide *feedback*. This can be defined as: acknowledging results and commenting on performance. There are a number of considerations to ensure the effectiveness of feedback.

- *All feedback must be accurate*. Saying nothing is better than giving incorrect information.

- *Always be positive*. Tell swimmers what to do, *never* just what not to do. An example might be: 'You showed an improvement in the length of pull, although it was still a little short. Now try to go all the way back to your thigh.' It is important to consider that unless you have a 'perfect' swimmer, it is usually possible to find something wrong with a stroke or skill. So, on occasion, it is a good idea to simply commend the improvement, to help boost confidence. The incorrect method would be to say something like: 'You are only pulling back as far as your waist. You must do better.' This not only fails to provide the necessary information for correcting the skill, it is also likely to damage confidence and morale.

- *Be specific*. Praise, such as, 'Well done, that was much better', is fine, but could be further improved by giving more information. For example, 'Much better, because your fingers were closed together this time.'

- *Try to encourage internal feedback*. 'Now you had your head back more, could you feel any difference?'

- *Whenever possible, give feedback as the swimmer performs*. You may have to provide feedback visually, as the swimmers are unlikely to be able to hear you. Give the 'thumbs up', or clap as they perform the required task. Also, give demonstrations in order to show some other requirement, or to reinforce the previous point.

- *Try to give feedback to as many swimmers as possible immediately after each practice*. Relate your feedback directly to the point being practised. Do not however overload yourself. It is better to give accurate feedback to two swimmers than to attempt to give inadequate feedback to four.

Swimmers – particularly children at primary school age – often want to please and to know how they are doing. Make sure you give positive feedback as much as possible. In addition, you may find that even very advanced swimmers require the reassurance of knowing that they are performing the skill as well as they might.

Manual Guidance

This form of communication has limited value for a number of reasons. Its use may contribute only a maximum of six per cent in the learning of a physical skill. It is best used with a pupil who is experiencing particular difficulties at attaining anything like the correct execution of the required skill – in spite of varying attempts at visual and verbal communication. The teacher may then, in this instance, manipulate the pupil's limbs through the correct movements. However, such a practice has a number of drawbacks, as follows.

- To activate a particular movement, a pupil's brain needs to be initiating the correct signals to the body's muscles. Because, in this instance, it is the teacher who is instigating the movements, such a process is unlikely to take place. In fact, the opposite effect is more likely – it is the teacher, not the pupil, who is being 'trained', in the skill of manipulation.
- The pupil will not be able to experience the pressure of the water and 'feel for the water' is what makes a swimmer successful.
- Quite often it will be impossible for the pupil to be in the correct plane, so that when they re-enter the water they will experience disorientation and confusion as to in which direction to move their limbs.
- The whole process of manual guidance is quite boring for a child (and potentially cold), since they would prefer to be in the water.
- It is possible for the teacher to transmit their frustration (through touch) at the pupil's inability to perform the skill.
- Unfortunately in today's society, it could be possible for a child to accuse a teacher of touching them in a manner which is

Fig. 2.21 *Manual guidance is not recommended by the ASA at this assistant teacher level*

unacceptable. All teachers should be wary, but it is fair to say that possibly, male teachers need to be more careful.

- Unless you are an octopus, it is only possible to offer manual guidance to one pupil at a time, thus cutting down on the use of valuable time. It also diverts your attention away from the rest of the class. This could result in other safety implications.
- It is quite possible that adult pupils would find it totally unacceptable for you to manipulate their limbs.
- You may physically injure someone if they resist the movements you are trying to make. It is for this reason that the ASA advises assistant teachers not to attempt manual guidance.

While it is accepted that for certain sports, manual guidance is a very useful form of communication, for swimming and associated skills it is usually regarded as the weakest of the three forms of communication. Use it only as a last resort and not before giving it great consideration.

Teaching Considerations
Acquisition of Skill

The major goal of your teaching should be: to help the swimmers achieve their maximum level of performance in all skills, in the shortest possible time and with the most enjoyment possible. This is achieved by considering the following.

- Give the maximum amount of opportunity for practise in the water. Dry land practice is of little value in acquiring a skill which is normally performed in the water.

- Ensure that appropriate amounts of rest are given, to enable the skill to be continued without deterioration of accuracy. The amount of rest required will vary depending on the level of the swimmer.
- The swimmer should experience success as often as possible. This is closely linked to the amount of rest that they are given and the distance that they have to achieve.
- You should offer praise whenever it is deserved, whether due to improved performance, increased effort or better behaviour. Even the latter will help in the quicker acquisition of skill.
- Give feedback – visually or verbally, or preferably both – whenever possible, as the swimmer is performing.
- Identify faults and good technique as quickly as possible. This is an ongoing process during any lesson. However, it may be necessary from time to time to perform a written analysis (*see* Chapter 1, page 8).
- Feedback must be positive. It must also be in direct relation to the aim of the lesson, and more often to the teaching point under consideration.
- Supply the necessary motivation, while ensuring that the pupil is not placed in a position which is too stressful.
- Set goals that are achievable.
- In your lessons or sessions, provide as much variety as possible with stimulating ideas.

Self-Evaluation
Evaluating Your Performance

As you can see from the list of teaching considerations, it is obvious that there is a great deal to consider in order to help pupils achieve their best. You are very unlikely to be able to carry out all the above in the early stages of your teaching career. Even when you are an established teacher you may from time to time slip into 'bad habits'. It is therefore essential to monitor your performance through ongoing self-evaluation. This should be carried out in two ways.

- Carry out an honest evaluation of your own performance as soon after you have taught as possible. If you use the sample evaluation in Chapter 3, page 30, you will be prompted in the right areas. It is an easy option to 'blame' a pupil for lack of achievement when in actual fact it may well be down to a fault of yours – for example, setting an unrealistic distance.

- Ask someone else to monitor your performance. This may happen automatically in some circumstances, for example: during any ASA teaching course; by your employer; by the teacher who you are assisting.

If you are to improve and progress you must continue to seek ways in which to achieve this. The feedback which you will receive should undoubtedly help to this end. Remember that your performance and reputation will often be measured by your swimmers' success (not necessarily their times or awards gained – often, their confidence, sense of self-fulfilment and improvements in technique).

Chapter 3
The Lesson/Session

Lesson Planning

During an ASA Assistant Teacher course, a number of the criteria that you must achieve relate to your ability to demonstrate 'Simple planning methods'. Especially in the early stages of the course, a good deal of the planning will be supplied by your course tutor. This will give you ample opportunity to observe the kind of details required.

Why Plan?

The principle reason for planning any lesson or session is to ensure that you are prepared. You will need to consider the following factors to ensure that you are fully prepared.

- The type of lesson. Is it to be an orthodox one (most course lessons are of this type), a stroke schedule lesson, a training schedule (for club swimmers), or a survival or recreational lesson?
- The number of swimmers. (On an ASA Assistant Teacher course, this should be a minimum of two and a maximum of four.)
- The time which you have available. Amongst other things, this will determine your selection of practices in relation to your aim.
- The space which is available to you. For example, do you only have width space, length space, shallow water, or deep water? Again, this will determine your selection of practices and how you might carry them out.
- The equipment which is available and how much you will need.
- The aim of your lesson.
- The ability level of the swimmers that you are working with.

There are a number of other reasons why planning is essential.

- In reality, after the course, the plan is likely to form part of a scheme of work. As such, it will form part of a term's work or a course of lessons. This may be your only opportunity to work on this particular stroke or skill during the course.
- The plan will also help to record work that you have carried out. It is essential therefore that you record such information as the date, the venue, and so on.
- It may be a prerequisite plan, in order for some subsequent skill to be taught.
- Your plan may contain skills which need to be taught so that a swimmer can attempt an award at the end of the course of lessons.

If you use the example session plan contained in your log book, and on the following pages, you will find that you are prompted into recording the necessary information. Planning takes practice and will be fairly time-consuming in the early stages.

The Session Plan

The following is a blank session plan as it appears in your log book (1999–2000). These formats are often reviewed and may change in minor detail, although remaining the same in principle. (*See* page 26 for advice on how to complete a session plan.)

AMATEUR SWIMMING ASSOCIATION

SESSION PLAN

This Session Plan should be used to record the lesson prepared for you by your Tutor/Supervisory Teacher

Name: . . . .

Class:	Date:	Time:	No. in Class:
Venue:		Length of Session:	Depth of Water:
Session Goal:		Ability:	

Equipment required:

Activity/Practices	Teaching Points	Organisation	Time

NB: **Please include references to any methods of entry and exits utilised during the sessions**

ASA ASSISTANT TEACHER CERTIFICATE LOG BOOK   April 1999
Section 3   Page

Table 3.1 *An ASA Assistant Teacher Certificate Session Plan*

Guide to Table 3.1: ASA Assistant Teacher Certificate Session Plan

Session details: See boxes at top of Table 3.1.

Class: Tadpoles, fishes, etc.
Date: Obvious
Time: Obvious
No. in class: 2–4

Venue: Location of the pool
Length of session: 20 mins, etc.
Depth of water: The range in your space

Session goal: Usually one of three statements: to improve, to revise, or to introduce. Then a specific aspect of one stroke, i.e. Back Crawl legs (dependent on the group's ability). Also include your contrasting activity, i.e. head-first sculling.
Ability: State this in relation to the particular goal of the lesson, i.e. if you are working on Front Crawl leg action, then state what their Front Crawl legs are like.
Equipment required: Be very specific as to what you will require, for example, ten floats and four sinkables (depending on the group's ability).

ACTIVITY/PRACTICES (SEE FIRST COLUMN)

You should split this area into three sections, remembering that there is another blank page accompanying this in your log book. All things written in this box are 'things to do'.

Introductory Activity

Intended as a warm-up. You do not necessarily have to attempt to teach anything. You may however relate this to your main theme or your contrasting activity if you wish, although it is not essential. *Example*: a running race over two widths.

Main Theme

Where you normally teach stroke work. Usually restricted to one stroke and, since time is limited (12 mins), often just one aspect of a stroke. *Example*: to improve Front Crawl leg action. The first and last practices are always whole stroke. The second activity should usually be a pupil demonstration, followed by another whole stroke practice. The successive practices are progressive part-practices. *Examples*: kicking at the rail; kick using two floats.

Contrasting Activity

Activities such as sculling, still using the same formula as in the main theme – whole skill, pupil demo, whole skill, part-practices, whole skill.

TEACHING POINTS (SEE SECOND COLUMN)

You should split this area into the same three corresponding sections. All things written in this box are 'things to think about' while doing the practice.

Introductory Activity

It is not necessary to have teaching points in this section, since the swimmers have just entered the water and their attention level may not be as high as it could be.

Main Theme

Each practice should be accompanied by only one point, which should be directly relevant to the aim of your lesson. *Example*: if your aim is to improve Front Crawl legs – kick your legs fast; make your legs long; have big floppy feet; point your toes. Remember that all points should be positive – don't use 'don'ts'.

Contrasting Activity

Points (things to think of) should be positive and directly relevant – for example, for sculling, wave at your feet.

ORGANISATION (SEE THIRD COLUMN)

Organisation is relevant to all three sections. You need to consider: space for individuals to perform in; time for a short rest between practices; that as much activity as possible is taking place; that your observational skills are not overloaded and that all participants are safe; that children do not become bored through lack of activity. Methods of organising are as follows:

- *Wave swimming* The first two swimmers set off. As they reach a given point, or on your command, the following two set off.
- *Cannon swimming* No. 1 swimmer sets off. No. 2 sets off at a given point, usually without your command, and so on.
- *Circuit swimming* Swimmers move in a chain formation around the area, instead of across widths.
- *Static practices* Either at the rail or in a suitable space.

You may also choose to organise the swimmers in other ways, but please remember that practices which involve only one performer at a time often lead to problems. Remember also to include in all sections how the pupils will enter the water – i.e. down the steps, slide in, jump in, dive in. Detail how they will exit – will they climb steps or over the side?

TIME (SEE FOURTH COLUMN)

The time spent on each activity in the three sections. Total time in this example is 20 mins.

Introductory
Since it is of little educational value, 3 mins.

Main Theme
Usually a minimum of 12 mins.

Contrasting Activity
Depends on the main theme.

Practical Teaching Considerations

- *Use the whole-part-whole method.* The swimmers attempt the whole stroke or skill; this provides the opportunity to practise the skill in its entirety. It also gives you the opportunity to check on their level of performance of the skill and select a pupil demonstrator if appropriate. Progressive part-practices are then used, interspersed with whole stroke or skill practices. This focuses their attention, and helps them to acquire particular parts of the stroke or skill. Finally, the whole skill is practised to give both teacher and swimmers the opportunity to monitor their improvement.

- *Give positive teaching points.* All the points which you ask them to 'think about' should be positive and directly relevant to your aim – in order to help them achieve the desired techniques.

- *Use the plan prepared* – either by you, or by your course tutor or lead teacher. Remember that the plan is a guide to what you expect to happen. If necessary, amend the plan or even disregard it. Teach the swimmers, not the 'plan'. If you do have to amend the plan in any way, it should be recorded in the evaluation.

- *Ensure a safe environment.* All practices performed, equipment used and behaviour should be safe for all.

- *Provide pupil demonstrations.* These help provide visual stimuli in relation to the skill being performed in its natural environment. They also have the effect of applying peer pressure.

- *Communicate and motivate*. Use ongoing verbal and visual communication, to motivate pupils by providing positive feedback and reinforcement.

Beginners' Guide to Conducting an Orthodox Swimming Lesson at Assistant Teacher Level

Before leaving home, check if you have your pool shoes, whistle, stopwatch, clipboard, log book, lesson plan and plastic wallet.

1 Arrive in plenty of time to either: liaise with your lead teacher; or be at your teaching station on an ASA course, and check the safety of the facilities and rescue equipment in your area.

2 Consult your lesson plan which may be either: prepared by you; or prepared by your ASA tutor or the lead teacher that you are assisting.

3 Get ready all the equipment that you require and position it safely.

4 Summon the children on to the poolside, or assist in this process if it is normally carried out by the ASA tutor or your lead teacher.

From this point on, it is assumed that you are 'working on your own' with a maximum of four children.

5 Greet the children, introduce yourself (if you are not known to them), do the register and discreetly check the children for their own safety. Long hair should at least be tied back; costume straps should be tied together behind the girl's back if they are loose; no excessively long Bermuda shorts; and no jewellery should be worn which could be either restrictive or get caught up

6 Give a brief explanation of your lesson aim.

7 Briefly set out your behavioural expectations.

8 Initiate the introductory activity or warm-up.

During points 9–18, remember that you should provide: one positive teaching point per practice; ongoing teacher demonstrations; and feedback, with occasional pupil demonstrations.

9 Whole stroke of the main theme (observe and select demonstrator, or borrow from another, more advanced group if necessary).

10 Pupil demonstration, with you providing a commentary.

11 Whole stroke practice of the pupil demonstration.

12 Progressive part-practices relevant to your aim (for example, legs-only practices), interspersed with the occasional whole stroke practice.

13 Final practice of the main theme should be whole stroke, so you can check on progress.

14 Whole practice of the contrasting activity (observe and select demonstrator, or borrow from a more advanced group if necessary).

15 Pupil demonstration, with you providing a commentary.

16 Whole skill practice of the pupil demonstration.

17 Progressive part-practices relevant to your aim.

18 Final whole skill practice of the contrasting activity, so that you can check on progress.

19 Swimmers leave the pool and gather around you. Summarise the lesson with a question-and-answer session.

20 Give brief information about your next lesson with them.

21 Escort them safely to the changing room entrance.

22 Sit down and have a stiff drink! You deserve it if no-one drowned, they listened, behaved well and performed to the best of their ability. Not much to it, is there?

23 When you have recovered, carry out an honest evaluation of the lesson, and record as necessary (badges passed, etc.).

If you follow this guide, in something resembling the same order, you will almost certainly be working on criteria relevant to the course.

Lesson Evaluation

Whenever you have taught during the course – whether the lesson plan has been prepared for you by the course tutor, or you have prepared it yourself – you should complete an evaluation as soon as possible afterwards (this again relates to the criteria given in Chapter 1, pages 2–3).

The example below is the type of form which you will find in your log book. As with the sample session plan, this is repeatedly reviewed. While there may be minor changes from time to time, the general principles will remain the same. (*See* pages 31–2 for advice on how to complete an evaluation.)

EVALUATION

1. **What was your Role within the context of the session?** e.g., responsible for a small group, taking a lane, team teaching?

2. **Pupils Performance** - e.g, in which aspects did the pupils improve?

3. **Content** - e.g., comments on the appropriateness/results of different practices

4. **Teaching** - e.g., reflect critically on 'your performance'. For example, your communication - were pupils clear what was expected? If pupils were not progressing, were you able to adapt what they were doing so that they could cope and improve? Organisation - was it effective? Did it allow pupils to participate fully and safely?

5. **Where there any behavioural difficulties?**

6. **Action Points:** List any action points for:

    •   Participants

    •   Yourself

7. **Miscellaneous** - e.g., any accidents/injuries?

Signed: . . . .

ASA ASSISTANT TEACHER CERTIFICATE LOG BOOK
Section 3

April 1999
Page

Table 3.2 *An ASA Assistant Teacher Evaluation*

A Guide to Table 3.2. An ASA Assistant Teacher Evaluation

1 What was your role within the context of the session? e.g. responsible for a small group, taking a lane, team teaching?

During a course your answer will usually be that you were responsible for a small group. Specify the number you had in the group. It may be that outside the course, you work in tandem with another teacher. In this case, you would answer 'team teaching' – and specify the teacher's name. If assisting outside the course, say whether you were assisting in the water. If so, was this for a particular section of the lesson; were you just providing participant demonstrations?

2 Pupils' performance – e.g. in which aspects did the pupils improve?

Relate this initially to the specific aim of the lesson then, to any other areas of practical performance. Finally, relate it to improvement in other areas (if any) – for example, behaviour, attentiveness, and so on. Be specific as to individual swimmers. This should not be difficult, since the maximum is four. *Example*: Ethel did improve her Front Crawl kick because she managed to keep it beneath the surface to a greater extent. Because she had a greater degree of success, she showed much more attention to me. Her ability to reach the pool floor only marginally improved, but she did at least completely submerge her head.

3 Content – e.g. comments on the appropriateness/results of different practices

Again, try to be specific as to individual swimmers. *Example*: Ethel adapted best to Front Crawl kicking when using two floats over one width. Kicking at the rail still resulted in her kicking out of the water, while when attempting to kick with only one float, she frequently had to stop due to the lack of support. When performing the contrasting activity, few practices had the desired effect due to her reluctance to submerge; she did however enjoy blowing bubbles.

4 Teaching – e.g. reflect critically on 'your performance'. For example, your communication – were pupils clear what was expected? If pupils were not progressing, were you able to adapt what they were doing so that they could cope and improve? Organisation – was it effective? Did it allow pupils to participate fully and safely?

Refer to page 7 in Chapter 1 (*Teaching and Coaching Analysis*) to prompt you. Ask the questions of yourself. Above all, it is very important to be totally honest with yourself if you are to gain any benefit from this exercise. When on a course, it is common for someone else to conduct an analysis of your performance; they may be able to help you to complete this section.

5 Were there any behavioural difficulties?

Again, be specific as to the individuals in your group. If there were any problems, you must ask yourself why. Was there too little activity? Were you sufficiently interested in them, and did it show? List in this section the actual problem; the reason for it may be linked to the section above on Teaching. It may of course be that the child did just behave badly, in spite of your best efforts! *Example*: Gertrude showed little attention to what was going on due to her interaction with Freda, who was continually splashing her. Albert was his usual angelic self, and so on.

6 Action points – list any action points for participants, and for yourself

Cover all aspects of the evaluation here: the practical content of the lesson; your performance; their behaviour. Again, since the maximum in the class is four, try to be specific as to individuals. *Example*: Ethel will need to spend a little more time developing the basics of Front Crawl kicking, and work much more on confidence. Albert is ready to progress to more advanced kicking practices. Gertrude and Freda need to be separated in the next lesson in the hope that they can concentrate a little better. I must remember to include more of my own demonstrations in the lesson (I will write them into my next plan).

7 Miscellaneous – e.g. any accidents/ injuries?

Hopefully, if you have been vigilant, then there will have been no injuries – although it is best to record anything, no matter how trivial it seems. If in doubt, consult a superior and fill in an accident report form. *Example*: Gertrude suffered a slight nose-bleed when Freda accidentally hit her with a crowbar. The bleeding soon stopped and she continued for the rest of the lesson with no further problem. If Gertrude and Freda continue to misbehave, I must remember to have a word with their parents.

Chapter 4
Health and Safety

Ensuring a Safe Environment

A swimming pool is without doubt a potentially very dangerous place, although if due respect is shown and simple rules and policies are observed, then the risk is minimised. It will be your responsibility to do everything in your power to prevent accidents from happening and to maintain a safe environment. As soon as you step on to a poolside, your prime concern should be the safety of both the pupils and yourself. It should remain so until all swimmers have left the poolside and you know that they are in the care of someone else.

Whenever you visit, work or assist at a different pool you should familiarise yourself with:

- the Normal Operating Procedure (NOP);
- the Emergency Action Plan (EAP).

The NOP

Contained within the NOP are all the details which relate to the day-to-day running of the pool. There are an enormous number of variables, due to the vast amount of different pools which are in use. Some of the most common include:

- the acceptable temperature range of both water and air;
- lifeguarding requirements in relation to the activity taking place;
- the acceptable bather load (the number of people in the pool at any one time – your class will be part of this);
- the responsibilities of different staff;
- the procedure for dealing with a variety of accidents or incidents;
- the qualifications required by staff, whether teaching or lifesaving.

This is by no means an exhaustive list. Always familiarise yourself with the NOP of individual pools.

The EAP

This always forms part of the NOP. Contained within the EAP are all the details which relate to dealing with an emergency of any description – not just drowning, but such things as gas leakage or fire. The exact details again depend on the pool, but the more common ones are:

- the emergency signal (this varies from pool to pool);

- the responsibilities of the different staff, for example the lifeguard, the swimming teacher, the visiting primary school teacher ;
- the location of all rescue aids;
- the location of other necessary equipment (phone, first-aid kit, etc.);
- the accident reporting system.

Having completely familiarised yourself with both the NOP and the EAP, you should set about establishing a regime of your own which complies with both. The following is an example.

- Ensure that you are safe by wearing appropriate footwear.
- Tie your hair back if it is long and interferes with your vision – for example, when bending down.
- Before allowing any pupils on to the poolside, check that all rescue equipment is where it should be and that it is functional. Check that any lifeguard cover is where it should be.
- Check that the pool is roped off as normal, if appropriate.
- Make sure you have any equipment you might require, so that you do not have to leave the pool. Ensure that it is stored on the poolside where it is not a danger to anyone and that it remains that way throughout the lesson.
- Check your numbers by going through the register if appropriate. Continually check throughout the lesson.
- Check the swimmers for their own personal safety. Long hair should at least be tied back; costume straps should be tied together behind the girl's back if they are loose; no excessively long Bermuda shorts; and no jewellery should be worn which could be either restrictive or get caught up.

- Check that swimmers who need medication have it with them (inhalers, etc.). Also ensure you are aware of any disabilities that may result in potential hazards, for example, a poorly sighted swimmer or someone who is hard of hearing.
- Boisterous behaviour is discouraged.
- Continually check that the swimmers are not showing excessive signs of fatigue which may result in them getting into difficulties.
- Also check that they are in an appropriate depth to perform the skill being carried out, and within a depth suited to their ability.

Finally, even though the authority at the pool where you work may not require you to have a life-saving qualification, you ought to have one – for peace of mind – and to ensure that you keep it up-to-date. There are a few available, some of which are specific to swimming teachers; and there are of course separate qualifications in First Aid and resuscitation. Techniques often change after careful review – keep yourself in the know!

Hygiene

Since swimming pools are used by vast numbers of people, it is imperative that we do as much as possible to ensure that the environment is as clean as possible and the risk of contracting an illness is minimised. As with safety (*see* pages 34–5), it is advisable to have a regime for hygiene.

- Check that very young swimmers have used the toilet before entering the pool and that they have also blown their nose.
- Check the cleanliness of the individual and their swimwear. (Be discreet while doing this; you do not want to embarrass the child and it may not be their fault.)

- If practicable, encourage the use of the shower before entering the pool.
- Long hair should ideally be contained inside a cap. Imagine how much hair is lost by 500 people in a pool in a day.
- Encourage the use of the toilet during a lesson especially for the very young (they may want to visit as many as three times in a lesson). Praise them on return for using the toilet; this will help encourage good habits.

You should also be careful to advise swimmers to refrain from taking part if they are suffering from a contagious disease or other affliction. Remember, we are not doctors and so should advise only. However, most people would be grateful if you suggested exclusion for the following:

- contagious diseases such as measles, etc;
- ear infections;
- open wounds;
- coughs and colds and other such ailments, especially if they are productive.

There are some conditions which have become stigmatised over the years, such as verrucae and athlete's foot. These are indeed contagious; however, recent opinion suggests exclusion is not necessary – especially since there are now treatments for verrucae which both cure the condition and form a seal over it to prevent it spreading. Remember that a swimmer would probably not be banned from a public swimming session for many of the above conditions. However, standards should not be lowered too much.

The Value of Swimming

Swimming has great value in our everyday existence.

Safety

- Since we inhabit an island, and our country has many inland waterways both man-made and natural, water safety needs to be an integral part of our education system.
- Fortunately, the National Curriculum now includes requirements in relation to swimming and water safety. Although numbers are dropping, somewhere in the region of between 500 and 800 people still drown in the UK each year.
- Everyone ought to be able to swim to minimise the danger both to themselves and to others.

Health and Fitness

With the advent of improved home entertainment and personal travel, it is quite probable that society as a whole is exercising less than it did in the not too distant past. For this reason, swimming has a great deal to offer.

- Age is not a restrictive factor in the pursuit of swimming. Older people who may not be able to exercise in any other way can usually still swim.
- It is a relatively cheap form of exercise, often being subsidised by local councils.
- Facilities are usually close at hand.
- People who suffer from some form of disability, and who may not be able to pursue other sports, can often swim due to the support that water offers.
- Swimming is often regarded as the complete exercise, helping individuals to develop their combined stamina, strength and suppleness to a greater extent than most other sports.
- Pregnant women can exercise right up to full term safely, while they might not be able to exercise in other ways.

- People who have suffered an injury can usually take part in an aquatic rehabilitation programme before they can rehabilitate in any other way.

Social Benefits

- Swimming is one of the few sports where all the family can participate together.
- Due to the fact that most pools are still public, it is quite probable that people have to socialise.

Access to Other Water Sports

Swimming is an essential skill for those people wishing to go on and participate in other water-based skills and sports. Some of these are more closely linked than others.

- Life saving
- Water polo
- Synchronised swimming
- Diving
- Aquafit
- Octopush
- Water-skiing
- Canoeing or boating
- Surfing
- Sub-aqua diving
- Wind-surfing and jet-skiing

Psychological Benefits

- Swimming is an excellent method of relaxing, both physically and psychologically. The swimmer is immersed and supported in a warm environment, a very good way of relieving stress.
- Participants, however young or old, can usually enjoy a degree of success and may even experience proven achievement by gaining a recognised award.

Chapter 5
The Non-Swimmer

Non-swimmers come in all ages, shapes and sizes, although it would be safe to assume that most who attend swimming lessons fall into the four- to eight-year-old range. (Adults will be dealt with as a separate entity.) Your ultimate aim should be to turn the non-swimmer into a confident swimmer in the shortest possible time.

Fig. 5.1 *Non-swimmers come in all ages, shapes and sizes*

There are a number of methods for teaching non-swimmers. Whichever method you are using, always remember the golden rule: with non-swimmers, you should assume that they know *nothing*, and that *everything* needs to be taught. Even simple skills such as how to enter the pool will need to be taught. If you use this approach the pupil is far more likely to have confidence and trust in you. Finally, you must be empathetic to the fact that they may be enduring both fear and embarrassment.

Fig. 5.2 *Even simple skills need to be taught*

Artificial Aids (worn aids)

This is probably the most popular method in use today.

- Artificial aids can be used in any depth of water, since the swimmer will be safely supported by at least one type of reliable aid. They are often used in conjunction with another type of aid. Worn aids should not however be considered a life-saving device. All aids should be comfortable, functional and fit securely to provide safety.

- The most common artificial aids are arm-discs or armbands, used in conjunction with a rubber ring for the more timid or less able. Arm-discs are very durable, since they cannot be punctured and can be removed one at a time as the swimmer progresses. They are generally available in only two different sizes, which slightly limits their usefulness for all non-swimmers. It normally takes three or four discs per arm to provide adequate support.

Fig. 5.3 *Pushing off from the rail should be avoided when wearing a rubber ring*

If a rubber ring is used, it must always be in conjunction with arm-discs to counteract the possibility of the ring being pushed around the swimmer's knees or feet. Pushing off from the rail or gutter should always be avoided, to help minimise this risk. Rings will always greatly assist a timid non-swimmer because of the higher position they provide. However, you should be attempting to increase confidence sufficiently to remove the ring and give a much more realistic position in the water. Rings should always be removed before arm-discs or armbands – never vice versa.

Pupils should be given regular opportunities to attempt swimming without buoyancy aids to ensure that they do not become dependent on them. These attempts must of course be made in safe conditions – i.e., in shallow water, or in deep water by the pool edge with a pole in front of them to hold if necessary.

Multi-Stroke Method

You would normally use this approach irrespective of whether swimmers are using worn or other buoyancy aids, and are in deep or shallow water. The multi-stroke approach should be used even when the non-swimmer has become a swimmer. Pupils should be given the opportunity to try out all stroke movements to find out which one they feel most comfortable with.

Over-the-water recovery movements should be avoided (*see* Fig 5.6, page 40) because:

* worn aids may become insecure;
* when swimming without aids, the pupil will not experience maximum buoyancy when a limb is lifted from the water.

Fig. 5.4 *Attempting to swim without buoyancy aids*

Fig. 5.5 *The multi-stroke method*

Fig. 5.6 *Over-the-water recovery movements should be avoided*

Fig. 5.7 *Discovery*

Focus on propulsive movements, such as the following.

- Front Crawl kick
- Front Paddle arms (an elongated, 'doggie-paddle' type of action)
- Back Crawl kick
- Back Paddle arms (pushing the hands backwards from level with the hips to the thighs)
- Simultaneous kicking
- Breaststroke arm pull

Pupils will usually need to use their arms, since in the early stages the leg action is likely to be ineffectual. Therefore, be considerate when using float practices for kicking. Some pupils may not move anywhere, causing failure for them and a potential problem for you.

Most practices will be of the 'whole' type to allow maximum practice and propulsion. A pupil may have most success by combining movements which are not usually associated – for example, Front Crawl legs and Breaststroke arms. This is perfectly acceptable if the desired end result – swimming without assistance – is achieved sooner rather than later.

Discovery

Children learn lots of skills through self-discovery. You should encourage this as much as possible. Give them every possible opportunity to move in different ways and directions. Use instructions like, 'See what happens if…' Ask them questions like 'Did you feel the difference when…?' or 'Can you do this?'

Water Confidence

Irrespective of any other method that you may be using, you should be trying continually to increase swimmers' confidence in the water. This usually results in quicker success. Activities aimed at increasing confidence should be included in most lessons, normally as:

- introductory or contrasting activities;
- occasionally, as the main theme.

Often, these activities are in the form of a game. You should try to make pupils *want* to do the activity, rather than feel that they have to do it. 'Put your face in the water and blow

Fig. 5.8 *Make the activity appealing*

bubbles' may appeal to some; but to others, it may be something that they would never contemplate. Instead, try something like this: ' You've all been to a drive-thru McDonald's. Now go to underwater-world McDonald's and order a Big Mac and chips.' Hopefully, they will be much more tempted to go underwater! Any activity that involves water around the face will be beneficial, especially if it is fun. Use stories to help.

Jumping In

Jumping in is a very useful and important skill and helps greatly to improve water confidence. When teaching jumping, be extra conscious of safety. Consider the following important points:

- toes over the edge to avoid slipping;
- look ahead, rather than down, to avoid overbalancing;

- bend knees to take off, and bend knees when landing in shallow water to avoid jarring the back.

If a child is timid you can follow two possible courses of action:

- have a helper in the water to 'catch them';

Fig. 5.9 *Jumping in*

- hold their hand as they jump and enter the water.

If using the second method, it is safer to do so at the corner of the pool. This way, the jumper can continue to face the correct direction, and you can avoid being pulled in. You might also use a pole for them to hold on to, instead of your hand. Irrespective of the method that you use, you should be trying progressively to reduce the amount of support required.

Shallow Water Method

Use only in 'special' pools, where the water is the same depth all over (approximately 18 in or 45 cm). This method is sometimes adapted for use in a lagoon-type pool at a leisure complex; or, for the large, wide steps which descend into some pools. Pupils would not normally wear buoyancy aids unless there is a chance of them straying into deeper water. They support themselves on their hands and 'crawl' around prone (face down) and supine (on the back), while at the same time kicking their legs in a horizontal position. This can progress to 'paddling movements'.

Teaching Adult Non-Swimmers

You will need first to consider carefully *why* such adults cannot swim. It is likely that fear, lack of experience and lack of opportunity for practice lie behind it. Therefore, empathy will need to be a key feature of your teaching. Adult non-swimmers may be embarrassed at not being able to perform skills which even young children can. They may also be embarrassed over their shape and the fact that they might be wearing buoyancy aids. To encourage them, use all the methods discussed so far. You may however have to adapt some of these, for example:

- you may find it more difficult to persuade an adult to swim in deep water;
- they may also already have a preference for one particular stroke (although they might have more success with a stroke they haven't yet tried);
- they could possibly have difficulty in performing some skills due to stiff joints;
- there will also be a greater percentage with poor eyesight and so will need even more reassurance from you.

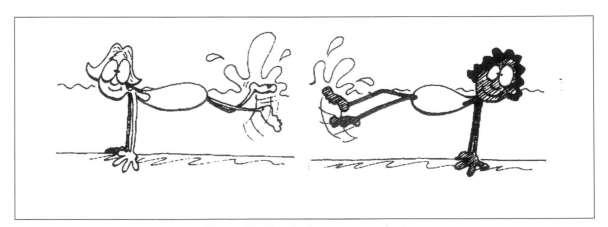

Fig. 5.10 *The shallow water method*

Remember to teach everything; assume they know nothing. They will not then have to admit that they don't know how to perform even a very simple skill.

Regaining the Standing Position (Adults)

It is possible that they will find this the most difficult skill.

It is also the one skill that greatly affects their confidence, although they may not be aware of how afraid they are at having to stop without the use of a rail. In my experience I have found that, for some reason, if a child is not swimming before about twelve years of age, they lose this ability to stand up after being horizontal. Younger children rarely have to be taught how to regain the standing position, they do it instinctively.

After establishing that the adult learner cannot stand up without assistance, set about teaching the skill from both the prone and supine position in order to increase their confidence. This will facilitate a more rapid acquisition of other skills. It will also make your job easier, since you will be able to use part-widths instead of always having to do full widths.

The skill of being able to stand from the horizontal position requires the co-ordination of three movements: lifting the head; pulling with the hands; and bringing

Fig. 5.12 *Regaining the standing position*

the legs under the body. Use rail exercises to practise these movements individually and together. Then, try the whole skill close by the rail. Since adults can usually be trusted, it is also possible to use partner support to help practise whole skills or part-skills.

Conclusion

Remember to praise adults just as much as you would children. Recognise every achievement to boost their confidence, and to prove to them that they are progressing – they may well have a negative attitude towards their own ability.

Fig. 5.11 *Regaining the standing position*

Fig. 5.13 *Use partner support*

Chapter 6
Scientific Principles of Swimming

It is essential that you understand why certain points of technique are desirable. Some children, and most adults, will ask you questions like, 'Why do I have to put my face in the water when I swim Front Crawl?' You will need to know about *floatation principles* (*see* pages 45–6) to answer them.

Fig. 6.1 *Floatation depends upon body density*

Scientific principles can be divided into three areas:

- factors affecting the way in which we float;
- factors affecting the different kinds of resistance we must overcome as we move;
- factors affecting how we move through water.

Floatation

Most humans should be able to float. Only a few will be unable to sustain a stationary floating position of some sort; although more will *think* that they are unable to float, particularly adult males.

The major factor which affects a human's ability to float is their density in comparison to the density of the liquid in which they are floating.

- Fresh water has a density of $1.0g/cm^3$.
- Salt water has a density of $1.024g/cm^3$.

Since the average male has a density of $0.98g/cm^3$, and the average female, $0.97g/cm^3$, it is clear that they should both float with a small amount of the body clear of the water's surface. This is usually the face, if floating in a supine position.

It is important to remember that a person's weight has little bearing on their density. It is almost certain, for example, that a female weighing 12 stone is less dense than a male weighing 9 stone. Other factors which affect the floating position are as follows.

- The amount of air in the lungs.
- The shape of the individual.
- A greater amount of fat in comparison to muscle and bone (this will reduce the density of the individual).
- The position of the centre of gravity.

Few adults can maintain a horizontal floating position in fresh water, especially males with little fat. They are far more likely to adopt an inclined position. Children of both sexes can usually float horizontally, or at least near-horizontally, especially when the arms and legs are spread in a star-type float. In addition, adult females have a greater chance of floating horizontally if they have a larger percentage of fat distributed around the hips and thighs.

Everyone should be able to float in the mushroom (jellyfish) float position (*see* Fig. 6.2, page 46; *see* also page 14), since it makes everyone the same shape and places the centre of gravity in the same position for all. Physical make-up has little bearing on this, unless they are extremely muscled.

Fig. 6.2 *Everyone should be able to float in the mushroom float position*

COMMON APPLICATIONS OF FLOATATION PRINCIPLES IN SWIMMING TEACHING

• Since only a maximum of three per cent of a human will float above the surface of fresh water, it is important that beginners keep all movements below the surface to keep them as buoyant as possible. Lifting limbs out of the water will only encourage sinking.

Fig. 6.3 *Keep all movements below the surface*

Fig. 6.4 *Maintain regular, even breathing*

Fig. 6.5 *Encourage a normal breath before a surface dive*

• Regular breathing is important, since while a continuous supply of air will help to keep a steady position, sudden exhalation of a large amount of air will only encourage a lower position. This can be particularly disadvantageous in Back Crawl.
• Don't ask a swimmer who is about to perform a surface dive to 'take a big, deep breath'. This can make it almost impossible to perform the dive, especially if the swimmer is a female with a greater percentage of fat. It is better to encourage a normal breath, and a gentle exhalation as they descend or swim forward under the water – ie. after the surface dive has been achieved.

Resistance

When human beings move through water, they will undoubtedly experience different forms of resistance to motion. Since we were not designed to travel through water, we must do everything to minimise resistance. There are three main forms of resistance, and one 'lesser' one. The three main ones are:

• profile resistance
• viscous drag
• eddy currents.

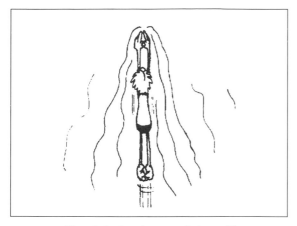

Fig. 6.6 *Good streamlining will minimise resistance*

Fig. 6.8 *Tighter clothing can help to streamline body shape*

Profile Resistance

This can be defined as: the resistance offered to forward motion by the shape of the swimmer, as he passes through water. Generally speaking, the narrower and smoother the shape, the lower the profile resistance – and the greater the ease of movement.

COMMON APPLICATIONS OF PROFILE RESISTANCE IN SWIMMING TEACHING

- As a swimmer pushes from the poolside, they should keep the arms together, the chin tucked in, and the legs together and in line with the rest of the body – thus minimising resistance. This is the essence

Fig. 6.7 *'Hunch' the shoulders in Breaststroke*

of good *streamlining*, which you should always aim for.
- 'Hunching' the shoulders in Breaststroke as the arms extend forward into the glide position will help to minimise the width of the body, thus reducing the profile resistance.
- A competitive, adult female swimmer may wear a costume which is very small to 'flatten' her chest, thus reducing her profile as she moves through the water.

Viscous Drag

When we move through water, it 'sticks' to us. There is friction between our skin and the water, and also between the water stuck to us and the surrounding water. This slows a swimmer down, just as any form of friction would any other kind of athlete.

COMMON APPLICATIONS OF VISCOUS DRAG IN SWIMMING TEACHING

- A swimmer with more body hair will experience more viscous drag (*see* Fig. 6.9, page 48), and so wearing a swimming hat – or, in extreme competition circumstances, shaving the body – helps to minimise this kind of resistance.

Fig. 6.9 *Body hair increases viscous drag*

Fig. 6.10 *Some swimming costumes are made of 'non-stick' material*

- Wearing a costume made of 'advanced' fabric helps to reduce the ability of water to stick to it. (Some costumes are even coated in Teflon – non-stick, just like frying pans.) These may also be designed to cover more of the body, even for males. They may cover as far down as the ankle, and up around the neck, with full sleeves as well.
- Cold water is more viscous, and so it is easier to swim through warm water.

Eddy Currents

As we move through water, it flows around the body. The smoother our shape, the more

Fig. 6.11 *It is easier to swim through warm water*

Fig. 6.12 *The effects of eddy currents*

easily water flows past, resulting in less turbulence behind. This turbulence is referred to as *eddy currents*, which 'drag' a swimmer. You can observe the effects of eddy currents by trying this little exercise.

- Stand waist-deep in water, holding a float flat and gently on the surface of the water. Walk backwards quite quickly and then gently let go of the float. The natural assumption is that the float will remain where it is. It will however follow you, even though you have lost contact with it.

The explanation is as follows: the water will have flowed past your back and sides and will form great turbulence (eddies) around your waist. It is this turbulence that drags the float along.

If you could extend a conical shape from your waist (rather like a competitive cyclist's helmet), the water would flow past easily and no eddies would be formed.

Eddy currents are strongly related to profile resistance. If profile resistance is good, eddies are minimised and drag is reduced.

COMMON APPLICATIONS OF EDDY CURRENTS IN SWIMMING TEACHING

- Anything that minimises profile resistance will automatically decrease the amount of eddy current resistance experienced.

The Drogue Effect

This lesser form of resistance is where an ill-fitting costume acts like an anchor and drags on the swimmer. Today, older boys and young adult males tend to favour 'Bermudas' over trunks; this greatly increases the drogue effect – and particularly when the shorts have pockets.

Fig. 6.13 *A conical shape such as this would eliminate eddy currents!*

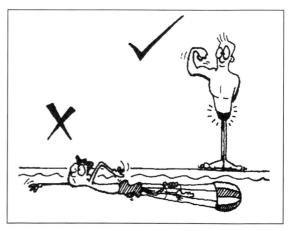

Fig. 6.14 *Ill-fitting costumes increase the drogue effect*

COMMON APPLICATION OF THE DROGUE EFFECT IN SWIMMING TEACHING

- If working with a competitive swimmer of school age, ensure that they wear tight-fitting swimwear to ensure maximum speed.
- When working with a swimmer who has to complete a distance award, ensure that they wear tight-fitting swimwear to enable them to swim further with the minimum amount of resistance.
- When working with competitive swimmers in training, encourage them occasionally to wear: ill-fitting swimwear; two costumes; a T-shirt or shorts; or a drag belt. This will have the benefit of making them work harder and improve strength; it will also make them appreciate the value of skin-tight swimwear.

Fig. 6.15 *Increasing the drogue effect can have training benefits*

Propulsion

We use a combination of two basic types of movement to propel ourselves through water.

- Paddling movements.
- Sculling movements.

Paddling Movements

Just as an oar is placed in the water and then pulled against it to move the boat forwards,

Fig. 6.16 *In Back Crawl, the forearm and hand act as an oar*

a swimmer may do the same in, for example, Back Crawl. It is important to realise the value that the forearm and a large flat hand can have in enabling the swimmer to 'catch' more water by increasing the size of 'their oar'.

This is classed as a *paddling movement*. It is in fact the less efficient method of the two, since the hand will move water backwards rather than move the swimmer forwards. This can be likened to a runner who attempts to move in sand. They will push sand backwards and traction will be decreased. The scientific theory which governs this kind of movement is Newton's third law of motion, which states that 'every action has an equal and opposite reaction'. Therefore, if you push back, you will move forward.

Sculling Movements

It is much more efficient to *scull* your way through water. This is achieved by ensuring that the hands in all strokes, and the feet in Breaststroke, move in a curved pathway. It has the added advantage of allowing the swimmer to pull against still water instead of water that they have moved (unlike the runner above, who is pushing against sand that they have moved).

The hands and feet are flatter on one side and more curved on the other. If they are moved in a curved pathway they 'part' the water. The water flows faster over the curved surface since it has further to travel, and the pressure is therefore reduced on this side. The swimmer will always move towards the area of reduced pressure. So, if the palms of the hands and soles of the feet always face backwards, then the swimmer will move forwards – even though they will not be moving hands or feet directly backwards.

The scientific theory which relates to this is Bernoulli's principle. The best example of this in relation to an aquatic skill is in head-first sculling. The hands are moved in a curved pathway (figure-of eight on its side) and never backwards. The palms face towards the feet. Movement takes place head-first, where the reduced pressure is – on the back of the hand.

Leverage

For all efficient movements in an aquatic environment, shorter levers are more advantageous than long ones.

Fig. 6.18 ... *than a short lever*

COMMON APPLICATIONS OF LEVERAGE IN SWIMMING TEACHING

- In Back Crawl, if a swimmer using the straight-arm pull (a long lever) applies a force of 130 pounds at his shoulder joint, then the resultant force at the hand is 10 pounds.
- If, however, he uses the bent-arm pull (shortening the lever with a 90-degree bend at the elbow), and exerts the same 130 pounds, then the resultant force at the hand is 16.25 pounds. A 62.5 per cent increase for the same effort.
- Even simple skills, like climbing out of the pool, are made easier by using bent arms (a short lever).

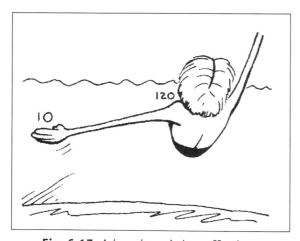

Fig. 6.17 *A long lever is less effective...*

The
Strokes

Chapter 7
Front Crawl

Front Crawl Technique
General Points

- Front Crawl is the fastest stroke for a number of reasons.
  - It is the most streamlined stroke.
  - It has the most continual propulsive output from the arm action, since one arm takes over propulsion before the other one finishes.
  - It places the body in the best position to apply a force from the strong groups of muscles in the chest, shoulders and back.
- There is no such recognised race as Front Crawl. However, it is usually used in Freestyle races.
- There are no laws relating to the performance of Front Crawl.
- It is the stroke most used in competitive swimming training, since there is less chance of injury.

Body Position

ESSENTIAL POINTS

1 The head should remain still, except when the swimmer is breathing. It should also be centrally positioned. Think of the head as the 'rudder', i.e. if the head is lifted, the hips drop. If the head is angled to the right, then the hips will deviate left, and so on.

2 The face should be submerged in the water approximately to the brow level – although this may change a little, depending on the build of the swimmer and also, in the case of competitive swimming, the distance being swum.

3 The eyes should look forwards and downwards.

4 The shoulders should be kept square to the direction of travel. They should also roll; this allows maximum force from the chest and back muscles, and also facilitates recovery of the non-propulsive arm.

5 The hips should be kept in line with the shoulders and close to the surface to allow for maximum streamlining.

6 The legs should also be kept in line with the body.

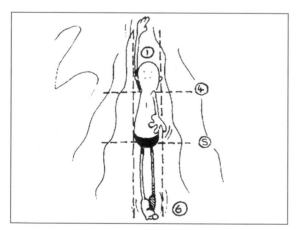

Fig. 7.1 *Front Crawl body position (a)*

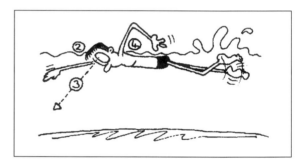

Fig. 7.2 *Front Crawl body position (b)*

Leg Action

The major function of the leg action is to balance the body position. The body would move around a great deal more in the absence of a leg-kick, due to the reaction of the arm action. The leg action also contributes to propulsion, although the extent of this contribution will vary quite dramatically depending on the level and skill of the swimmer. Generally, the more advanced the swimmer, the less propulsion from the leg-kick; this is because the arm action will have been refined and is much more capable of a large propulsive output. Almost all of the propulsion which is achieved by the leg action is derived from the downward kick.

ESSENTIAL POINTS

1   The kick is continuous and alternating, although a distance swimmer or highly buoyant swimmer may use a two-beat leg-kick instead of a six-beat kick. (A beat is defined as the number of kicks per one complete cycle of the arms.)

2   The kick should be initiated in the hip.

Fig. 7.3 *Front Crawl leg action (a)*

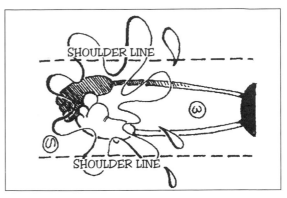

Fig. 7.4 *Front Crawl leg action (b)*

3   The legs should pass close by each other, knees almost knocking.

4   The feet should be stretched away from the knee, toes pointed (*plantarflexed*).

5   Turning the feet inwards is highly desirable (*intoeing*).

6   The ankles should be loose and flexible.

7   The sole of the foot should reach the surface on the upward kick but should not break the surface of the water.

8   A bend in the knee will be required in order to produce some propulsion on the downward kick; however, this should not be stressed. The impression should be of a stretched leg.

9   The depth of the leg-kick should be preferably within that of the body position, since any deeper would adversely affect streamlining.

Arm Action

Almost all the propulsion in Front Crawl is generated by the arms. The arm action is highly efficient, but should be very relaxed, particularly during the recovery phase.

ESSENTIAL POINTS
Entry

1 This should be as 'clean' as possible; splashing should be avoided.

2 Fingertips first with the thumb-side down, palm facing outwards. The usual angle in relation to the surface of the water is around 45 degrees.

3 The fingers should be almost together with a fairly flat palm.

4 It should be at a comfortable stretch (4A) anywhere between the centre line of the body and the shoulder line on the side of the entering hand (4B). The elbow should be higher than the hand on entry (4C).

Propulsive phase

Generally speaking, the hand will follow the pathway of an elongated 'S' shape.

1 After entry, the hand travels forwards to a comfortable stretch.

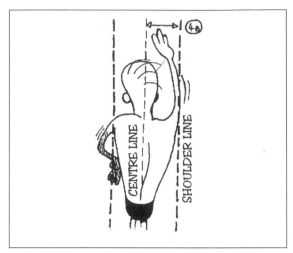

Fig. 7.6 *Front Crawl arm action – entry (b)*

2 From this point onwards, throughout the propulsive phase, the palm faces in the same direction that the hand is travelling, in addition to always facing predominantly backwards.

3 Without pausing, the hand sweeps downwards and slightly outwards to exert a feeling of pressure on the palm (*catch*).

4 It continues to sweep downwards and outwards until approximately level with the line of the shoulder on that side of the body.

5 The elbow should be kept high to enable good leverage.

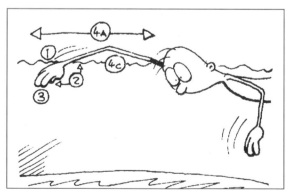

Fig. 7.5 *Front Crawl arm action – entry (a)*

Fig. 7.7 *Front Crawl arm action – propulsive phase (a)*

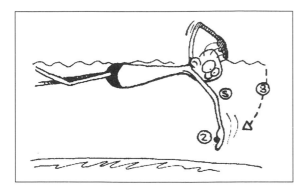

Fig. 7.8 *Front Crawl arm action – propulsive phase (b)*

Fig. 7.10 *Front Crawl arm action – propulsive phase (d)*

6   The hand now sweeps inwards towards the centre line of the body. It will have reached the centre line when approximately level with the shoulder. The elbow will now be bent to a maximum of 90 degrees.

7   From this point on, the hand sweeps upwards and outwards as the arm extends and the hand reaches the thigh.

8   There is gradual and continual acceleration throughout the whole phase.

Recovery phase

1   Before leaving the water, the palm will smoothly rotate to face the thigh.

2   The whole recovery should be as relaxed as possible.

3   The elbow leaves the water first and is lifted sufficiently to allow the fingertips to be clear of the water.

4   The elbow then travels forwards with the arm kept as close to the body-line as possible.

5   When approximately level with the shoulder, the hand travels forwards to the entry point (but with the elbow always higher).

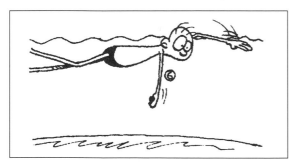

Fig. 7.9 *Front Crawl arm action – propulsive phase (c)*

Fig. 7.11 *Front Crawl arm action – recovery phase*

Breathing Technique

ESSENTIAL POINTS

The timing of the breathing technique as it corresponds with the arm action is as follows.

1   As one arm has made the initial downsweep in the propulsive phase, the shoulder on that side will be rolling downwards and the opposite shoulder will be lifting upwards.

2   This is an optimum time to turn the head towards the lifting shoulder for inhalation, as the arm on that side is recovering.

3   The face is returned to the water as the recovering arm is approximately level with the shoulder.

4   Inhalation can take place with the mouth still half in the water, since the general level of the water is lower around the mouth. (This is known as the '*bow wave*'.)

Exhalation can take place in one of two different ways, as follows.

5   *Trickle breathing*, where air is gradually and continually exhaled during the whole time that the face is in the water.

6   *Explosive breathing*, where the breath is held while the face is in the water and is then forcibly exhaled just as the mouth breaks the surface.

Quite often, these two methods are combined; air is gently trickled out and then, as the face turns, a final and forced exhalation is made.

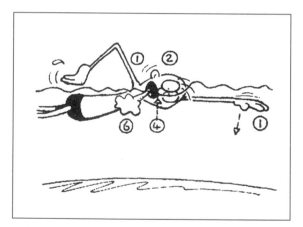

Fig. 7.12 *Front Crawl breathing techniques (a)*

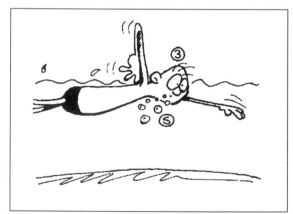

Fig. 7.13 *Front Crawl breathing techniques (b)*

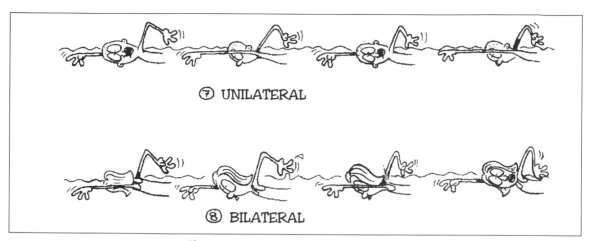

⑦ UNILATERAL

⑧ BILATERAL

Fig. 7.14 *Front Crawl breathing patterns*

Breathing patterns

The most common patterns of breathing are shown in Fig. 7.14.

7 *Unilateral*, where the head is turned to breathe either every complete cycle of the arms, or every two complete cycles. This results in breathing taking place to one side only.

8 *Bilateral*, where the head is turned to breathe either every one-and-a-half cycles of the arms, or every two-and-a-half cycles of the arms. This results in breathing taking place to both sides.

Co-ordination

ESSENTIAL POINTS

There are usually six beats of the legs per arm cycle. This may change — depending on the distance being swum — to four or even to two. Some more buoyant swimmers may also use between two and four beats.

Front Crawl Practices

The following are suggested practices for teaching Front Crawl. Please be aware that this is not an exhaustive list and you should try other practices if you feel that they would be of benefit to swimmers. Research other publications for further ideas.

When selecting practices, bear in mind that the lower the level of the swimmer, the shorter the distance normally practised. This is to ensure success, and to prevent the skill from breaking down. The higher the level of the swimmer, the greater the need to practise over a longer distance. This will enforce a skill in a stroke which will already have been practised extensively and therefore will be 'inbred'. Remember, however, to continually provide the opportunity to succeed.

Generally, teach in the following order: body position, leg action, arm action, breathing technique, timing. Always consider that each element does not have to be 'perfect' but must have a degree of consistency and solidarity before progressing to the next. Also remember that a few aspects of each element may be interdependent – i.e., a certain degree of aquatic breathing is required to maintain a good body position. All the following are part-stroke practices which are progressive.

Body Position

STATIC PRACTICES

1 While standing in shallow water, shoulders under, slowly submerge the face to brow level (Fig. 7.15).

2 Holding the gutter, submerge the face brow level while extending the arms and legs (Fig. 7.16).

Fig. 7.15 *Front Crawl body position – static practices (a)*

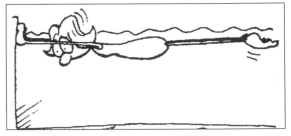

Fig. 7.16 *Front Crawl body position — static practices (b)*

Fig. 7.17 *Front Crawl body position — static practices (c)*

3 Floating in shallow water, prone and extended, submerge the face to brow level while holding two floats and progressing to one float (Fig. 7.17).

4 Floating prone and extended with no floats, submerge face to brow level (Fig. 7.18).

Fig. 7.18 *Front Crawl body position – static practices (d)*

MOVING PRACTICES
Preferably, these are all performed with the face in the water.

5 While holding an appropriate number of floats, push and glide from the wall by pushing against the wall with one foot (Fig. 7.19).

6 Standing a few paces from the wall, shoulders under and arms extended, submerge face then push to the gutter rail. Increase the distance as required until a kick would be needed in order to reach the gutter rail (Fig. 7.20).

Fig. 7.19 *Front Crawl body position – moving practices (a)*

Fig. 7.20 *Front Crawl body position – moving practices (b)*

Fig. 7.21 *Front Crawl body position – moving practices (c)*

7 Standing with the back to the wall, shoulders submerged. One foot pushes against the wall to glide (Fig. 7.21).

8 Holding the gutter rail, both feet against the wall and shoulders in (this could be taught as a skill in itself). Hands slide forwards and under to a stretch, then push until the whole body is stretched (Fig. 7.22).

Fig. 7.22 *Front Crawl body position – moving practices (d)*

Leg Action
STATIC PRACTICES

1 Sitting on the edge of the pool, kick feet to make a small splash (Fig. 7.23).

2 Overgrasping the gutter, with extended arms and face in the water, kick for varying lengths of time without inducing stress (Fig. 7.24).

Fig. 7.23 *Front Crawl leg action – static practices (a)*

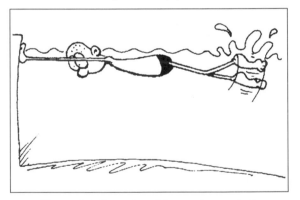

Fig. 7.24 *Front Crawl leg action – static practices (b)*

MOVING PRACTICES

Preferably, these are all performed with the face in the water – with the exception of (3).

3   With a float in each hand, supporting each elbow, and placed under the chin, kick for a short distance. Gradually increase the distance (Fig. 7.25).

4   With two floats 'sandwiched' together and arms extended, kick for a short distance. Gradually increase the distance (Fig. 7.26).

Fig. 7.28 *Front Crawl leg action – moving practices (d)*

Fig. 7.29 *Front Crawl leg action – moving practices (e)*

5   With one float and arms extended, kick for a short distance. Gradually increase the distance (Fig. 7.27).

6   Standing about five paces away from the wall, push and glide (Fig. 7.28. *See also* Fig. 7.20), and then kick. Gradually increase the distance until a breath would be required to be able to reach the gutter rail.

7   Push and glide as shown in Fig. 7.22, then kick. Gradually increase the distance until a width is achieved (Fig. 7.29).

Fig. 7.25 *Front Crawl leg action – moving practices (a)*

Fig. 7.26 *Front Crawl leg action – moving practices (b)*

Fig. 7.27 *Front Crawl leg action – moving practices (c)*

Developing strength in the leg action
These practices are used once the kick is accurate.

8 Kick over widths, with the float vertical to provide a resistance (Fig. 7.30).

9 Kick with no floats as in Fig. 7.29, over multiple widths.

10 Kick with one float around a circuit, or circuits (Fig. 7.31).

Fig. 7.30 *Front Crawl leg action – developing strength (a)*

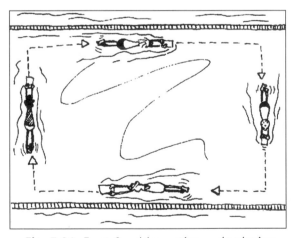

Fig. 7.31 *Front Crawl leg action – developing strength (b)*

Arm Action

Due to the balancing effect of the leg action, it is important to remember that a reasonable kick should be achieved before moving on to work on the arm action. Consider also that, often, too much emphasis is placed on the entry and recovery of the arm action and insufficient work is done on the propulsive phase as a result. Propulsive efficiency will eventually lead to proficiency in the water. Some aspects of the recovery are also difficult to perform without a good propulsive phase. For example, unless the propulsive phase is long, it is unlikely that the swimmer will be able to recover without 'dragging'. Having stated these facts, the recovery and entry phases should not be neglected since, similarly, some aspects of efficient propulsion depend on these.

STATIC PRACTICE

1 Standing in shallow water, one foot further forwards than the other and shoulders and face in the water, practise the full arm action (Fig. 7.32).

Fig. 7.32 *Front Crawl arm action*

MOVING PRACTICES

2 Elongated front paddle practice (Fig. 7.33).

3 As Fig. 7.32, but walking.

4 As Fig. 7.29, adding one complete cycle of the arms when approximately half-way across the width. Continue kicking to the other side (Fig. 7.34).

5 As practice (4) above, but with two arm cycles and gradually increasing when more proficiency is demonstrated.

6 Single-arm practices can also be used, but bear in mind that some children may be too small to hold a float at the front edge and still have room for their face. They may also lack the strength necessary for rolling the body when

Fig. 7.35 *Front Crawl arm action – moving practices (c)*

Fig. 7.36 *Front Crawl arm action – moving practices (d)*

using a float in this manner. Consequently, the practice may have to be performed without the float – or be amended to exclude the roll (Fig. 7.35).

7 Perform the arm action while using a pull-buoy. Remember that this should only be attempted by more proficient swimmers (Fig. 7.36).

Fig. 7.33 *Front Crawl arm action – moving practices (a)*

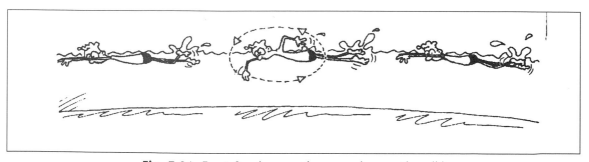

Fig. 7.34 *Front Crawl arm action – moving practices (b)*

Breathing Technique

Breathing in a controlled, regular manner is quite a complex skill and is therefore best left to a later stage. All swimmers should already have by this stage a correct appreciation of exhalation into the water. However, they probably cannot co-ordinate the breathing technique with their arm action.

STATIC PRACTICES

1   Hold the pool rail with one arm extended and the other arm by the side, feet on the floor, body piked at the waist. Practise breathing to the side (Fig. 7.37).

2   As in practice (1) above, but with an extended kicking position (Fig. 7.38).

3   Standing in shallow water, practise the arm action while using both unilateral and bilateral breathing – two, three or four strokes.

MOVING PRACTICES

4   As practice (3) above, but walking.

5   Holding a float at each end, kicking and breathing as necessary using the preferred technique (Fig. 7.39).

6   As with practice (5) above, but turning to look at a partner as they travel across (Fig. 7.39).

Fig. 7.37 *Front Crawl breathing technique – static practices (a)*

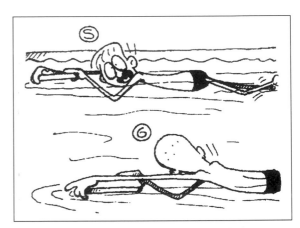

Fig. 7.39 *Front Crawl breathing technique – moving practices (a)*

Fig. 7.38 *Front Crawl breathing technique – static practices (b)*

Fig. 7.40 *Front Crawl breathing technique – moving practices (b)*

Fig. 7.41 *Front Crawl breathing technique – moving practices (c)*

7 One arm extended in front, one by the side (Superman pose), kick and breathe as necessary using preferred technique (Fig. 7.40).

8 Push, glide, kick, arm action and breathe once across the width. Stand if and when necessary (Fig. 7.41).

9 As practice (8) above, increasing the number of breaths per width.

10 As practice (9) above, but for lengths or circuits.

A range of Front Crawl skills and drills for the more advanced swimmer are included in Chapter 12 on competitive swimming training.

Front Crawl Teaching Points

Remember that each time the swimmer performs a practice, they should be given a point of technique to think about (the *teaching point*). Each teaching point should be positive and as stimulating as possible. You should endeavour to expand your repertoire of points as much as you can; this will greatly enhance your teaching success. A sample of the more common points, both formal and more imaginative, are listed below.

Body Position

- Make yourself as long as you can.
- Try to lie flat at the surface of the water.
- Put your forehead in the water.
- Pretend you are Superman, flying as stretched as he does.
- Pretend you are made of rubber and someone is pulling you at both ends.
- Keep your eyes open as you look for mermaids.

Leg Action

- Kick your legs fast all the time.
- Kick from your bottom.
- Stretch your legs out as much as possible.
- Keep your knees close as you kick.
- Point your toes away from you.
- Make your ankles 'wobbly'.
- Try to make a little splash with your toes.
- Pretend your ankles are made of jelly.
- Pretend you are trying to kick off your wellies.

Arm Action

- Keep your arms moving all the time.
- Put your fingertips in the water first.
- Keep your fingers together.
- Make your hand as flat as a pancake.
- Make your hand draw a big long 'S' under the water.
- Brush your hand past your thigh.
- Bend your arm gradually as you pull under the water.
- Lift your elbow out of the water first.
- Make your hand go faster from going in the water to leaving it.
- Keep your elbow high as your arm goes over the water.

Breathing

- Blow out slowly into the water.
- Turn your head to the side to take a breath.
- As you pull with one arm, turn your head to the other side to breathe in.
- Turn your head back into the water as your arm comes over.

Front Crawl Faults

Each person's interpretation of the 'desired Front Crawl technique' will differ, so that they will swim the stroke in a slightly different way. This is known as an individual's 'style'. However, there are specific aspects of Front Crawl performance which are categorically wrong. These can be referred to as *faults*.

Listed opposite are the more common faults, but the list is by no means exhaustive. When trying to remedy a fault, it is important to identify the cause by carrying out a stroke analysis (see pages 8–9). Once the cause is identified, select a simple practice and appropriate teaching point to help the individual achieve the desired technique.

Body Position

- Failure to submerge the face to brow level.
- Moving the head from its central position.
- Not keeping the whole body in a straight line.
- Insufficient rolling of the shoulders.
- Too much inclination from head to toes.

Leg Action

- Kicking from the knee.
- Overbending the legs.
- Shaking rather than kicking the legs.
- Keeping the ankles too stiff.
- Having the legs too far apart.
- Making too much splash.
- Failing to make the feet reach the surface.
- Dorsiflexing the feet.
- Not kicking continuously.

Arm Action

- Keeping the fingers too wide apart and also cupping the hand.
- Lack of pulling back to the thigh.
- Failure to accelerate through the pull.
- Keeping the arms too straight under the water.
- Entering the hand wide of the shoulder line or across the centre line.
- Pulling across the centre line or wide of the shoulder line.

Breathing

- Holding the breath.
- Going too long without a breath.
- Turning the head to breathe too early or too late.

Laws of the Sport

Please note that it is not necessary to know the numbers of the laws. These are referred to only for reference to their inclusion in the ASA publication, *The Laws of the Sport*. They are edited to include only the information required for the ASA Assistant Teacher (Swimming) course. Further information on the laws concerning Starts, Turns and Finishes would be given on a teacher course. It is important to remember that knowledge of the laws is not only necessary for competitive purposes, but also in relation to many ASA awards. Finally, please note that there are no specific laws relating to Front Crawl – only to Freestyle, the event in which it is normally swum.

Freestyle

512.2 Freestyle means that in an event so designated, the swimmer may swim any style; except that in Individual Medley or Medley Relay events, Freestyle means any style other than Backstroke, Breaststroke or Butterfly.

Chapter 8
Back Crawl

Back Crawl Technique
General Points

- Back Crawl is the third fastest stroke.
- It is rarely used in competitive training due to the risk of collision.
- Back Crawl is the stroke used in Backstroke races.
- It is advantageous for beginners since the face is kept clear of the water.
- A disadvantage of the stroke for all swimmers is general disorientation and a fear of 'banging into the side'.

Body Position

ESSENTIAL POINTS

1 The body should be kept as streamlined as possible. Sideways movement of the legs should be avoided.

2 When viewed from the side, the ideal impression is of a shallow saucer from the head to the toes. This means that the hips are a little lower to allow the up-kick to stay beneath the surface.

3 The body should be kept in a supine position, although the shoulders should roll up and down (about the longitudinal axis). This will allow for a stronger pull and an easier recovery of the arms.

4 The head will be still, with the eyes looking upwards and very slightly towards the wall that the swimmer is leaving – at about the join of the wall and ceiling.

5 The head should be kept in a central position.

6 The waterline should be 'cutting' the ears with an impression of the head being 'pillowed'.

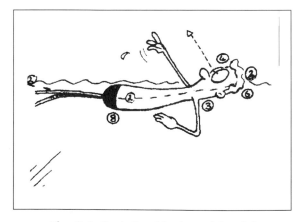

Fig. 8.1 *Back Crawl body position (a)*

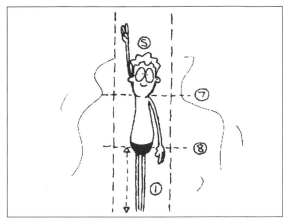

Fig. 8.2 *Back Crawl body position (b)*

7 The shoulders should remain square to the direction they are facing.

8 The hips will also roll about the longitudinal axis. Both the hips and legs should remain in line with the rest of the body to maximise streamlining.

Leg Action

The major function of the leg action is to balance the body position as a result of the reaction to the movement of the arms. (A simple test to prove this is to swim Back Crawl using a pull-buoy between the thighs. The legs will deviate laterally a great deal. When the pull-buoy is removed and the leg-kick added, deviation is minimised.) The leg-kick will also contribute to propulsion, although this will vary quite dramatically depending on the level and skill of the swimmer.

ESSENTIAL POINTS

1 The legs should kick alternately and continuously.

2 The kick should initiate in the hip.

3 The legs should pass close by each other, with an impression of the knees almost knocking.

4 The feet should be stretched away from the knee, toes pointed (*plantarflexed*).

5 Turning the feet inwards is highly desirable (*intoeing*).

6 The ankles should be loose and flexible.

7 On the upward kick, the toes should reach but not break the surface. Only a small splash should be created.

8 A bend in the knee will be required at the beginning of the upward kick in order to produce some propulsion. However, this should not be stressed. The impression should be that of a stretched leg.

9 The leg will be predominantly straight on the downward kick, due to the force of the water acting on the back of the leg and knee joint.

10 The leg-kick should not be too deep in order to ensure good streamlining – although, to be efficient, it will have to move up and down quite significantly. The depth will be in proportion to the size of the swimmer.

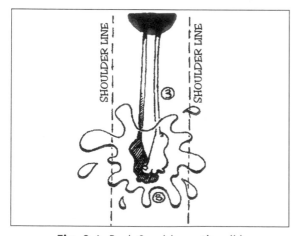

Fig. 8.3 *Back Crawl leg action (a)*

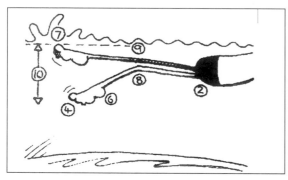

Fig. 8.4 *Back Crawl leg action (b)*

Arm Action

Most of the propulsion derived in Back Crawl is generated by the arm action. Ability to perform the bent-arm pull will assist greatly to this end – this will depend on the level of the swimmer. Whether using the bent-arm pull or the straight-arm pull, the recovery should be as relaxed as possible.

ESSENTIAL POINTS

The arms should move alternately and continuously.

Entry

1 Usually made with the little finger first.
2 The hand should be flat with the fingers very close together or closed.
3 The arm should be straight and preferably in line with the shoulder with the palm facing outwards

Fig. 8.5 *Back Crawl arm action – entry (a)*

Fig. 8.6 *Back Crawl arm action – entry (b)*

Fig. 8.8 *Back Crawl arm action – bent-arm pull*

Propulsive phase

1   Whichever pull is used, the propulsive phase is from entry to the exit point at the thigh. The action accelerates throughout.

Straight-arm pull

It may be necessary to use this with less skilled swimmers in the early stages. However, you should attempt to introduce the bent-arm pull as early as possible.

2   From entry, the straight arm sweeps in a semi-circle through 180 degrees, close to the surface of the water until it reaches the thigh.

Bent-arm pull

1   If viewed from the side, the general impression should be of the hand following the path of an 'S' on its side.

2   After entry, whichever direction the hand travels in is the direction the palm should face, in addition to always facing predominantly backwards.

Downsweep

1   Without pausing, the hand sweeps downwards and outwards to exert a feeling of pressure on the palm (*catch*).

2   The shoulder will roll towards this arm.

3   The arm will begin to gradually bend at the elbow.

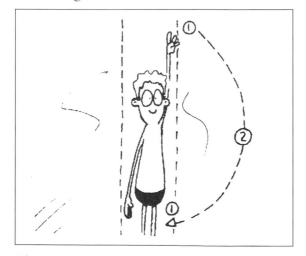

Fig. 8.7 *Back Crawl arm action – propulsive phase*

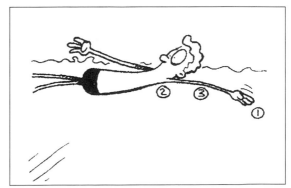

Fig. 8.9 *Back Crawl arm action – downsweep*

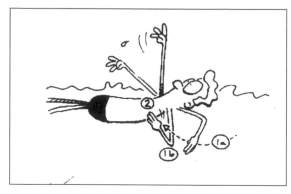

Fig. 8.10 *Back Crawl arm action – upsweep*

Upsweep

To continue travelling down and out would greatly affect streamlining and fail to use the propulsive actions efficiently.

1a Before the hand reaches shoulder level, it begins to sweep inwards and upwards.

1b It will have reached its highest point by the time it is level with the shoulder (elbow bend will be at 90 degrees, with the hand fairly close to the surface).

2 The hand is now at the top of the S shape on its side.

2nd Downsweep

1 The hand sweeps inwards and downwards towards the thigh and the floor of the pool.

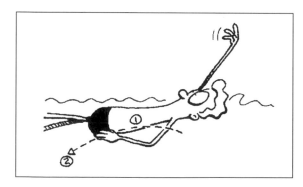

Fig. 8.11 *Back Crawl arm action – 2nd downsweep*

2 The action will be complete when the arm is fully extended with the palm facing downwards just below the hip.

Recovery phase

1a Before leaving the water, most swimmers will rotate the palm to face the thigh, making a thumb-first exit.

1b However, some may relax the wrist and exit back of the hand first.

1c A few may rotate the back of the hand to face the thigh and therefore exit little finger first.

2 Whichever method is chosen, lifting the shoulder before the hand leaves the water will put the body in a more streamlined position and ensure that the arm does not displace water straight into the swimmer's face.

3a The arm is lifted straight over the shoulder in a relaxed manner and travels through 180 degrees.

3b At approximately the 90-degree position, the arm is rotated at the shoulder to prepare for entry of the little finger.

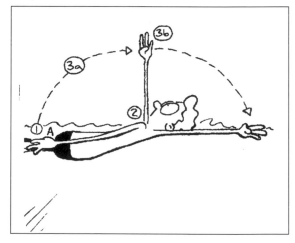

Fig. 8.12 *Back Crawl arm action – recovery (a)*

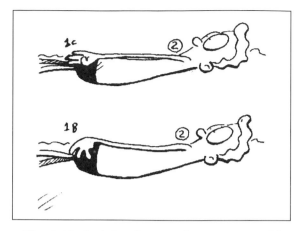

Fig. 8.13 *Back Crawl arm action – recovery (b)*

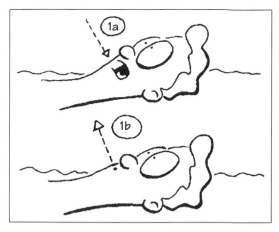

Fig. 8.15 *Back Crawl breathing technique (b)*

Breathing Technique

ESSENTIAL POINTS

Normal breathing should be encouraged.
Some swimmers may choose to:

1a breathe in as one arm recovers;

1b breathe out as the other arm recovers.

Co-ordination

ESSENTIAL POINTS

There are usually six beats of the legs per arm cycle. The arms always act completely in opposition – i.e., as one hand enters, the other will be exiting.

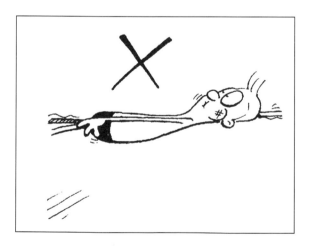

Fig. 8.14 *Back Crawl breathing technique (a)*

Back Crawl Practices

The following is a list of suggested part-stroke practices for the progressive teaching of Back Crawl. This list will give you sufficient ideas for an ASA Assistant Teacher course (*see* also Chapter 12 on 'drills' for the competitive swimmer). If you already have ideas or practices which are not included in this list, by all means try them – but bear in mind the following:

- the less advanced the swimmer, then usually, the shorter the distance practised. This ensures success, and prevents the skill from breaking down;
- the more advanced the swimmer, the greater the need to practise the skill over a longer distance to enable improvement.

Whatever you practise with the swimmers, remember that you should always be aiming to optimise their chances of success.

Always use the whole-part-whole approach and, when teaching the 'part' elements, try to teach in the following order:

- Body position
- Leg action
- Arm action
- Breathing technique
- Co-ordination

While doing this, bear in mind that it is not necessary for each element to be 'perfect' before progressing to the next – though a degree of consistency and solidarity is required. Remember also that a few aspects of each element are interdependent, for example, the leg-kick must reach the surface of the water in order for a reasonable body position to be achieved.

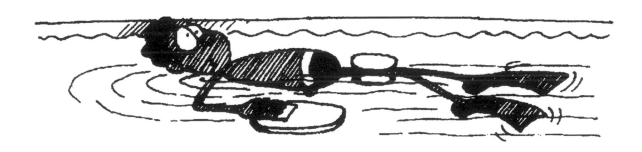

Body Position

STATIC PRACTICES

1 Hold the rail, shoulders under the water and feet on the wall – toes just under. Practise putting the head back with the ears in the appropriate position (Fig. 8.16).

2 With feet hooked under the rail and arms supported by a float under each arm, practise stretching the whole body, again with the head back (Fig. 8.17). (This is only possible if you have a rail instead of a gutter.)

3 As in practice (2) above, but floating free of the rail (Fig. 8.17).

4 As in practice (3) above, but with one float on the chest; this gives a more streamlined position with less dependency on aids (Fig. 8.18). This practice may

Fig. 8.18 *Back Crawl body position static practices (c)*

Fig. 8.19 *Body Crawl body position – static practices (d)*

sometimes be performed with the float held on the stomach or thighs to provide support if the swimmer is finding maintaining a horizontal position difficult – or if they are bringing their knees out of the water. The swimmer may also hold the sides of the float instead of crossing their arms over it.

5 As in practice (4) above, but with no float to increase confidence and to prove ability to float (Fig. 8.19).

Fig. 8.16 *Back Crawl body position – static practices (a)*

Fig. 8.17 *Back Crawl body position – static practices (b)*

MOVING PRACTICES

1 With shoulders submerged and head back, and supported by a float under each arm, practise pushing from the wall into a stretched supine position (Fig. 8.20).

2 As in practice (1) above, but with one float on the chest to reduce dependency on aids (Fig. 8.21). The float may also be held in the different ways stated in static practice (4).

3 Start in the position shown in Fig. 8.16. Release the rail but keep arms submerged. Gently push against the wall with the feet until a moving, stretched position is achieved (Fig. 8.22).

4 As in practice (3) above, but push a little harder to achieve a greater distance (set distance targets, perhaps).

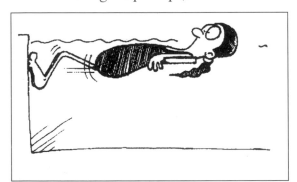

Fig. 8.20 *Back Crawl body position – moving practices (a)*

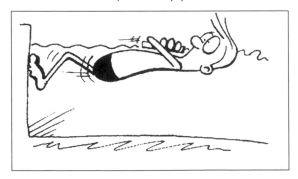

Fig. 8.21 *Back Crawl body position – moving practices (b)*

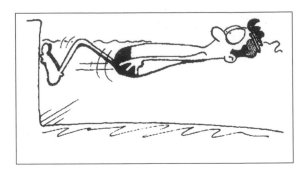

Fig. 8.22 *Back Crawl body position – moving practices (c)*

Leg Action

STATIC PRACTICES

1 Sitting on the edge of the pool, 'dangle' feet or legs in the water and practise kicking (Fig. 8.23).

2 If a deck-level pool is being used, rest head on poolside – and possibly the arms – and practise kicking in a more stretched position (Fig. 8.24).

Fig. 8.23 *Back Crawl leg action – static practices (a)*

Fig. 8.24 *Back Crawl leg action – static practices (b)*

MOVING PRACTICES

1 As in Fig. 8.20, practise kicking for short distances. Distances should be increased as the swimmer improves (Fig. 8.25).

2 As in Fig. 8.21. Once the swimmer is showing proficiency in practice (1) above, use this over short distances (which again should increase as the swimmer improves) (Fig. 8.26).

3 As in Fig. 8.22. Use the same procedure, starting with a short distance and increasing this as the swimmer becomes more proficient and confident. Initially, it may be necessary to use a paddling action of the arms for assistance (Fig. 8.27).

Fig. 8.27 *Back Crawl leg action – moving practices (c)*

Fig. 8.25 *Back Crawl leg action – moving practices (a)*

Developing strength in the leg action

These practices should be used once the kick is accurate.

1 Use body position moving practice (3) (Fig. 8.22), but throw the arms over the water until the body is stretched (Fig. 8.28). The hands are together, just under the surface and the arms stretched. Practise kicking, usually over longer distances.

2 Use a float as a resistance, held in the same position as the hands in practice (1) above. The float needs to be semi-submerged and in a vertical position (Fig. 8.29).

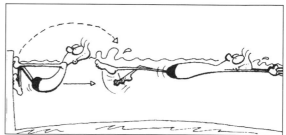

Fig. 8.28 *Developing strength in the Back Crawl leg action (a)*

Fig. 8.26 *Back Crawl leg action – moving practices (b)*

Fig. 8.29 *Developing strength in the Back Crawl leg action (b)*

Arm Action

Due to the balancing effect of the leg action, it is important that the swimmer achieve a kick which maintains a horizontal position before moving on to work on the arm action. Bear in mind also that equal emphasis should be placed on the three phases of the arm action:

- Entry
- Propulsive phase
- Recovery

STATIC PRACTICES

1 Standing, practise the arm action emphasising continuity and a long action (Fig. 8.30). (This practice is of limited value and should be kept short.)

Fig. 8.30 *Back Crawl arm action – static practice*

Fig. 8.31 *Back Crawl arm action – moving practices (a)*

MOVING PRACTICES

1 Start as in Fig. 8.22. Add leg-kick and – at a given point across the width – add one complete cycle of the arms (Fig. 8.31). Gradually increase the number of cycles as the accuracy increases.

2 Start as in Fig. 8.21. Add leg-kick – practise single-arm Back Crawl (Fig. 8.32). Keep distances short and change arms frequently. (Please note that for some swimmers using a float may impair the stroke if the float inhibits their ability to roll the shoulders. If necessary, allow them to practise without.)

3 Use a pull-buoy between the thighs and perform the arm action (Fig. 8.33). Start with short distances and gradually increase.

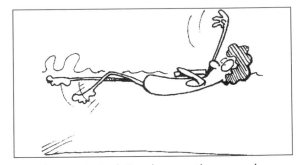

Fig. 8.32 *Back Crawl arm action – moving practices (b)*

Fig. 8.33 *Back Crawl arm action – moving practices (c)*

Breathing Technique

While it should not be necessary to devise specific practices for this, you should ensure that swimmers breathe normally, particularly in the early body and leg action practices. As the swimmer progresses you may need to teach the pattern of breathing 'in on one arm and out on the other'. It should only be necessary to do this if it is apparent that the swimmer is not breathing regularly, or if they are having difficulty with water around their face. Use short distance, full-stroke practices to achieve this.

Co-ordination

Again, it should not be necessary to devise specific practices for co-ordination if in the early stages of your teaching you have placed sufficient emphasis on continuity. Use short distance, full-stroke practices to emphasise and ensure continuity. More Back Crawl skills and drills are included in Chapter 12.

Back Crawl Teaching Points

Remember that each time swimmers perform a practice, they should be given a point of technique to think about (the *teaching point*). Each point should be positive, relevant to your aim and as stimulating as possible. You should endeavour to expand your repertoire of points as much as possible; this will greatly enhance your teaching success. A sample of the more common teaching points – both formal and informal – are listed below.

Body Position

- Make yourself as long as you can.
- Keep your head back.
- Look up and slightly towards your toes.
- Keep your head still.
- Roll your shoulder towards the arm that you are pulling with.
- Pretend you are lying in your bed and your head is on your pillow.
- Keep yourself in a big, long, straight line.
- Pretend you are sunbathing and trying to get your tummy tanned.

Leg Action

- Kick your legs fast all the time.
- Kick from your bottom.
- Stretch your legs as much as possible.
- Make your toes 'bash into' each other.
- Try to make the water boil with your toes.
- Keep your knees close by each other.
- Pretend you are a ballerina; point your toes.
- Turn your toes in towards each other.

Arm Action

- Keep your arms moving all the time.
- Make your hand stretch all the way behind you.
- Put your hand in the water in line with your shoulder.
- Put your little finger in the water first.
- Keep your fingers closed together.
- Try to draw a letter 'S' on its side, under the water.
- Make your hand go all the way back to your thigh.
- 'Zoom' your hand through the water.
- Lift your thumb out of the water first.
- Make your arm go upwards over your body.

Breathing

- Breathe normally.
- Breathe in as one arm enters the water and out as the other one enters.

Back Crawl Faults

Each person's interpretation of 'the desired Back Crawl technique' will differ, so that they will swim the stroke in a slightly different way. This is known as an individual's '*style*'. However, there are specific aspects of Back Crawl performance which are categorically wrong. These can be referred to as *faults*.

Listed below are the more common faults, but the list is by no means exhaustive. When trying to remedy a fault, it is important to identify the cause by carrying out a stroke analysis (*see* pages 8–9). Once the cause is identified, select a simple practice and relevant teaching point to help the individual achieve the desired technique.

Body Position

- Keeping the head out of the water.
- Not stretching the body, sinking the bottom.
- Keeping the eyes closed.
- Failing to keep the body in a straight line.
- Moving the head about.
- Swimming with the head not in its central position.

Leg Action

- Kicking from the knee.
- Over-bending the legs.
- Having the legs too far apart.
- Shaking rather than kicking the legs.
- Failing to make the feet reach the surface.
- Making too much splash.
- Not kicking continuously.
- Turning the feet outwards.
- Failing to relax the ankles.

Arm Action

- Not moving the arms continuously, often resulting in 'pausing' at the thigh.

- Entering the arms too wide.
- Entering the arms over the centre line.
- Having the fingers wide apart or hands cupped.
- Pulling too deep.
- Failure to pull all the way through to the thigh.
- Lack of acceleration through the pull.

Breathing

- Holding the breath.

Laws of the Sport

Please note that it is not necessary to know the numbers of the laws. These are referred to only for reference to their inclusion in the ASA publication, *The Laws of the Sport*. They are edited to include only the information required for the ASA Assistant Teacher (Swimming) course. Further information on the laws concerning Starts, Turns and Finishes would be given on a teacher course. It is important to remember that knowledge of the laws is not only necessary for competitive purposes, but also in relation to many ASA awards.

Backstroke

515.2 At the signal for starting and after turning, the swimmer shall push off and swim upon his back throughout the race except when executing a turn as set out in ASA technical rule 515.4. The normal position on the back can include a roll movement of the body up to, but not including 90 degrees from the horizontal. The position of the head is not relevant.

515.3 Some part of the swimmer must break the surface of the water throughout the race.

Chapter 9
Breaststroke

Breaststroke Technique
General Points

Breaststroke is the slowest stroke due to a number of factors:

- it is the least streamlined stroke
- recovery of the arms is usually under the water
- there is a short period during the stroke where no propulsion is occurring from either arms or legs
- the length of pull of the arms is relatively short.

There are more laws relating to Breaststroke than the other strokes, and it is used less frequently during competitive training for the following reasons:

- the risk of injury to others
- stress on the swimmer's joints, resulting from the 'unnatural' movements of the limbs.

Finally, it is the oldest competitive stroke – Captain Matthew Webb swam the English channel in 1875 using Breaststroke!

Body Position

Breaststroke is swum in a variety of ways, particularly in a competitive environment. There are however some critical points, irrespective of the style being swum; *streamlining* should be of prime concern.

ESSENTIAL POINTS

1   There must be a 'slope' from shoulders to hips to allow the leg-kick to stay beneath the surface. (This slope may be quite severe in the 'High style' or 'Dolphin style' of Breaststroke; the swimmer will still however be in a streamlined position.)

2   The head should be centrally positioned.

3   Some swimmers may hold the head completely out of the water (3a),

Fig. 9.1 *Breaststroke body position (a)*

Fig. 9.3 *Breaststroke body position (c)*

although it is more desirable to submerge it to brow level (3b). (The 'High style' swimmer may submerge the head completely (3c) though to comply with ASA law some part of it must break the surface during each stroke cycle.)

4   The head should be held still. (The 'High style' swimmer may nod the head a little as they extend the arms forwards.)

5   The eyes should look forwards and downwards.

6   The shoulders should be parallel to the surface of the water.

7   The hips should be parallel to the surface of the water.

Fig. 9.2 *Breaststroke body position (b)*

Leg Action

Unlike in the other three strokes, the major function of the Breaststroke kick is to provide propulsion. It has little, if any, balancing effect. Some older people may swim in a style which is now rarely taught, known as the 'wedge kick' (a wide, poorly streamlined action).

The Breaststroke kick can be broken down into two phases.

ESSENTIAL POINTS

Recovery phase

1 The kick starts with the legs extended and together.
2 The heels part a little and are drawn to the seat.
3 The knees point downwards and stay almost still – behind the swimmer – as the feet move towards the seat, soles up.
4 The knees should stay around the width of the hips to maximise streamlining.

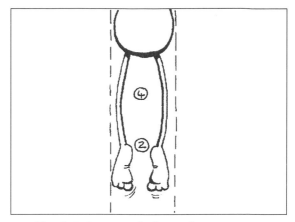

Fig. 9.5 *Breaststroke leg action – recovery phase (b)*

5 Once at the seat, without pause, the feet turn towards the knee (*dorsiflex*) and also turn out (this is again to comply with ASA law, as well as being desirable – *see* page 100).

6 The feet are now ready for the propulsive phase. If viewed from behind at this stage, the swimmer's legs would form a 'W' shape.

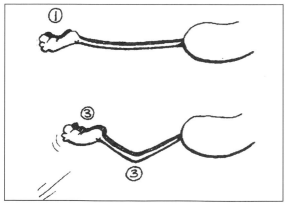

Fig. 9.4 *Breaststroke leg action – recovery phase (a)*

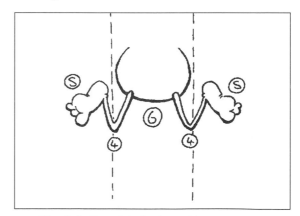

Fig. 9.6 *Breaststroke leg action – recovery phase (c)*

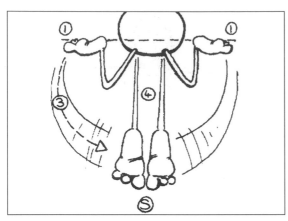

Fig. 9.7 *Breaststroke leg action – propulsive phase (a)*

Propulsive phase

1   To comply with ASA law the feet should be in the same horizontal plane as each other and remain so throughout the whole action (*see* page 100).

2   The action will accelerate throughout.

3   The feet sweep out and down in an 'arc-like' shape. (The width of this will vary between swimmers, although it is desirable to keep it fairly narrow for streamlining.)

4   The legs continually and gradually extend.

5   The feet sweep and 'drive' inwards to meet at full extension, when they will be plantarflexed.

Fig. 9.8 *Breaststroke leg action – propulsive phase (b)*

6   The feet and legs may now naturally rise towards the surface – although to comply with ASA law, this cannot be in the form of a kick (*see* page 100).

Arm Action

There is less propulsion generated by the arm action than in the other three strokes. The arm action is performed in a variety of different styles; there are however some common points .

ESSENTIAL POINTS
Propulsive phase
'Out and down' sweeps

1   Generally speaking, the palm will face in the same direction as the hand is travelling, in addition to predominantly facing backwards.

2   The action will accelerate throughout the stroke.

3   To comply with ASA law, the arms must move simultaneously (*see* page 100).

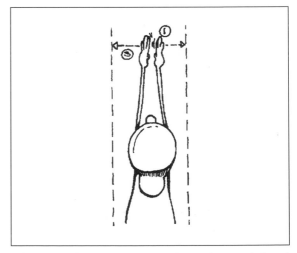

Fig. 9.9 *Breaststroke arm action – 'out and down' sweeps*

Fig. 9.10 *Breaststroke arm action – 'out and down' sweeps*

Fig. 9.11 *Breaststroke arm action – insweep*

4 From an extended position just below the surface, the hands are angled outwards at approximately 45 degrees, with the palms almost flat and the fingers almost together.

5 The hands sweep out and slightly downwards to approximately shoulder-width apart. This is to gain a feeling of the pressure of the water (*catch*).

6 They then sweep further downwards in an 'arc-like' shape with the elbows kept high and bending gradually to assist leverage and gain maximum 'catch'.

Insweep
1 The hands now sweep inwards towards the centre line of the body. They may also sweep upwards towards the surface.

2 The elbows should also move inwards, to 'tuck' into the sides in preparation for a streamlined recovery.

Recovery phase
The hands can recover in a variety of ways, although whichever method is chosen, it must be from the breast to comply with ASA law (*see* page 100).

1 The hands will be close together, almost touching.

2 The most common way in which to recover the hands is just below the surface, palms down.

3 A 'High style' swimmer may recover with the palms facing each other, or even palms uppermost. They may also recover through the surface or even over the water.

4 The hands move forwards until the arms are fully extended.

5 There may now be a short glide. Competitive swimmers will minimise or even exclude the glide.

Fig. 9.12 *Breaststroke arm action – recovery*

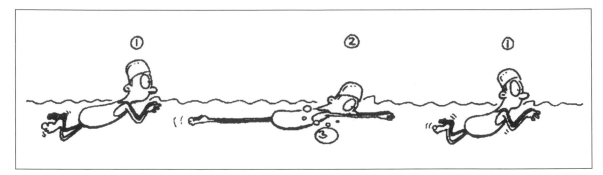

Fig. 9.13 *Breaststroke breathing technique (a)*

Breathing Technique

ESSENTIAL POINTS

The position of the head will vary depending on the style being swum. Some swimmers may have their chin in the water as they inhale, while others in the opposite extreme may have their chin as much as 30 cm above the surface.

Fig. 9.14 *Breaststroke breathing technique (b)*

1 A breath is usually taken every stroke cycle.

2 As the hands sweep inwards, the body will be at its highest position, irrespective of the style being swum. Inhalation should therefore take place at this point.

3 The face is returned to the water (if this is the style being swum) as the arms are extending forwards from the breast.

4 The swimmer can either 'trickle breathe' while the face is in the water, or breathe out explosively just as the mouth is surfacing. Some swimmers may even combine the two methods.

Co-ordination

ESSENTIAL POINTS

The timing is quite straightforward and logical. It is usually summarised as Pull–Breathe–Kick–(Glide).

1 The arms *Pull* (the legs will 'trail' to maximise streamlining).

2 *Breathe* (the head will be at its highest position after pulling).

3 *Kick* (the feet will be at the seat to take over propulsion after the pull has finished).

4 *Glide* or stretch (the arms extend forwards for streamlining as the legs kick).

Fig. 9.15 *Breaststroke co-ordination*

Breaststroke Practices

The following is a list of suggested part-practices for the progressive teaching of Breaststroke. This list will give you sufficient ideas for an ASA Assistant Teacher course. (*see* also Chapter 12 on 'drills' for the competitive swimmer). It is not an exhaustive list, so if you already have ideas or practices which are not included, please try them. However, bear in mind the following:

- the less advanced swimmer will practise over a shorter distance, and the more advanced swimmer over a longer one;
- always optimise the chances of success.

Generally, try to teach in the following order:

- Body position
- Leg action
- Arm action
- Breathing technique
- Co-ordination

However, since the leg action is more complex than that for the other three strokes, it is accepted procedure to teach the arm action alongside the leg action.

Always bear in mind that each element does not have to be perfect but must have a degree of solidarity and be consistently performed before progressing to the next. Also, remember that a few elements may be interdependent – for example, the arm action will need to be symmetrical for an even body position to be maintained.

Fig. 9.16 *Breaststroke body position – static practices (a)*

Body Position

STATIC PRACTICES

All practices should emphasise level shoulders and hips. In the early stages, they may be performed with the chin resting on the water instead of with the face submerged.

1   While standing in shallow water, submerge the shoulders and then slowly submerge the face to brow level (Fig. 9.16).

2   Holding the rail, submerge the face to brow level while extending the arms and legs (Fig. 9.17).

3   Floating in shallow water – prone and extended with the face in at brow level – hold two floats and progress to one (Fig. 9.18).

4   Floating prone and extended with no floats, lift the chin forwards (Fig. 9.19).

Fig. 9.17 *Breaststroke body position – static practices (b)*

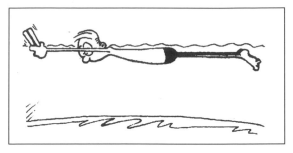

Fig. 9.18 *Breaststroke body position – static practices (c)*

Fig. 9.19 *Breaststroke body position – static practices (d)*

MOVING PRACTICES

1   Standing a few paces from the wall, with shoulders under and arms extended, submerge the face and then push to the poolside. Increase the distance gradually until a propulsive movement of some description would be needed (Fig. 9.20).

Fig. 9.20 *Breaststroke body position – moving practices (a)*

Fig. 9.21 *Breaststroke body position – moving practices (b)*

Fig. 9.23 *Breaststroke leg action – static practices (a)*

2 Stand with back to the wall, shoulders submerged. One foot pushes against the wall to glide away (Fig. 9.21).

3 Hold the gutter or rail with both hands, both feet against the wall and shoulders in (this could be taught as a skill in itself). Slide hands forwards under the water to a stretch, then push until the whole body is stretched and the glide position is achieved (Fig. 9.22).

Leg Action
STATIC PRACTICES

1 Sitting on the pool edge, attempting the kick, swimmers observing their own actions (please note that their feet should be in the water in order for them to be able to 'feel' the resistance offered by the water. Dry land practices have little value) (Fig. 9.23).

2 Holding the rail or gutter with elbows and forearms resting against the pool wall, practise the recovery element only (Fig. 9.24).

Fig. 9.22 *Breaststroke body position – moving practices (c)*

Fig. 9.24 *Breaststroke leg action – static practices (b)*

Fig. 9.25 *Breaststroke leg action – static practices (c)*

Fig. 9.27 *Breaststroke leg action – static practices (e)*

3 As in practice (2) above, but include dorsiflexing and turning the feet out when the feet are at the seat (Fig. 9.25).

4 Repeat practice (3) above, now including the propulsive phase. Do one kick initially, then have a short rest. Then, kick more continually but always sufficiently slowly to enable maximum concentration (Fig. 9.25).

5 Holding the rail or gutter in slightly deeper water, practise kicking in a vertical position (Fig. 9.26). (The force of

the water on the sole assists with dorsiflexing).

6 With a float under each elbow in slightly deeper water, practise kicking in a vertical position (Fig. 9.27).

MOVING PRACTICES

1 With a float held under each elbow and the chin resting on the surface, kick and gradually increase the distance (Fig. 9.28). (This practice can also be performed in a supine position.)

Fig. 9.26 *Breaststroke leg action – static practices (d)*

Fig. 9.28 *Breaststroke leg action – moving practices (a)*

Fig. 9.29 *Breaststroke leg action – moving practices (b)*

2   Sandwich two floats to provide support. Kick and gradually increase the distance (Fig. 9.29).

3   With one float, kick and gradually increase the distance.

4   Start as in Fig. 9.22 then push and glide. Perform an arm pull then kick and glide (Fig. 9.30).

5   Repeat practice (4) above, increasing the number of cycles.

Developing strength in the leg kick

These practices should only be used once the kick is accurate.

1   Push, glide – leaving the arms extended – and kick. Gradually increase the distance (Fig. 9.31).

2   Push, glide then bring the hands back to the seat with the palms facing rearwards. Attempt to kick the palms with the heels to ensure a complete recovery of the feet and maximum power (Fig. 9.32).

Please note that practices (1) and (2) above can be quite stressful on the spine and so periods of practise should be kept short and not performed too often.

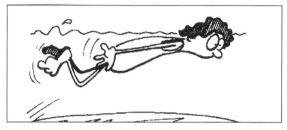

Fig. 9.32 *Developing strength in the Breaststroke leg-kick (b)*

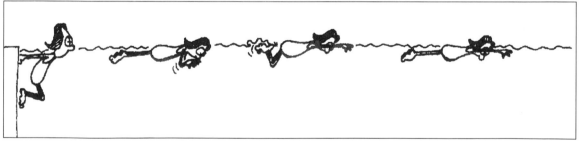

Fig. 9.30 *Breaststroke leg action – moving practices (c)*

Fig. 9.31 *Developing strength in the Breaststroke leg-kick (a)*

Fig. 9.33 *Developing strength in the Breaststroke leg-kick (c)*

Fig. 9.34 *Breaststroke arm action*

3 Kick with a float held in a vertical position, half in the water, half out to act as a resistance (Fig. 9.33).

Arm Action

STATIC PRACTICE

1 Standing in shallow water with the shoulders submerged, swimmers practise the arm action while copying the ongoing demonstration (supplied by you). The arm action can be heavily broken down into the sweeping movements – i.e. the outsweep – and then progressing to each subsequent stage until the action is complete (Fig. 9.34).

MOVING PRACTICES

1 As the static practice, but walking (Fig. 9.34).

2 Push and glide and add one or two arm actions (Fig. 9.35).

3 Swim arms only, with a pull-buoy between the thighs (Fig. 9.36). (This should only be used with more advanced swimmers.)

Fig. 9.35 *Breaststroke arm action – moving practices (a)*

Fig. 9.36 *Breaststroke arm action – moving practices (b)*

Fig. 9.38 *Breaststroke breathing technique – static practices (b)*

Breathing Technique

STATIC PRACTICES

1 Stand in shallow water leaning forwards. Practise exhaling into the water and pushing the chin forwards to inhale (Fig. 9.37).

2 As practice (1) above, co-ordinating with the arm action (Fig. 9.38).

MOVING PRACTICES

1 As in Fig. 9.38, walking (Fig. 9.39).

Fig. 9.39 *Breaststroke breathing technique – moving practices (a)*

Fig. 9.37 *Breaststroke breathing technique – static practices (a)*

2 Push, glide – then pull, breathe and stand (Fig. 9.40).

3 As practice (2) above, but continue swimming instead of standing.

Co-ordination

1 Push and glide – then pull, breathe, kick and glide, then stand (Fig. 9.41).

Breaststroke Teaching Points

Remember that each time a swimmer performs a practice, they should be given a point of technique to think about (the *teaching point*). Each point should be positive, relevant to the lesson aim and as stimulating as possible. You should endeavour to expand your repertoire of points as much as possible; this will greatly enhance your teaching success. Below are listed a sample of the more common Breaststroke teaching points – both formal and more imaginative.

Fig. 9.40 *Breaststroke breathing technique – moving practices (b)*

Fig. 9.41 *Breaststroke co-ordination*

Body Position

- Keep your head still.
- Keep your shoulders level.
- Make your hips slightly lower than your shoulders.
- Pretend you are carrying a precious cargo on your back; keep your shoulders flat so that you don't tip it off.
- Keep your hips level.

Leg Action

- Kick your legs simultaneously.
- Keep your legs level with each other.
- Try to kick your seat with your heels.
- Keep your knees fairly close together.
- Turn your feet out sideways.
- Bend your big toes up towards your knee-cap.
- Kick back and around powerfully.
- Pretend you have got penguins' feet.
- Kick like a frog.
- Make sure your feet meet at the end of your kick as your legs are fully stretched.

Arm Action

- Move both your arms simultaneously.
- Make your hands draw the shape of an upside-down heart.
- Keep your elbows high as you pull.
- Keep your fingers closed together and palms nearly flat.
- Pretend you are scraping out the sides of a pudding basin.
- Stretch your arms forwards until they are straight.
- Tuck your elbows in by your sides after you have pulled.
- Keep your hands under the water as you pull.

- Make your hands come together by your chest.
- Speed up your hands as you pull.

Breathing and Co-ordination

- Breathe in as you are finishing pulling and out as you stretch forwards.
- Pull your arms, then breathe, kick and finally stretch.

Breaststroke Faults

Each person's interpretation of 'the desired Breastroke technique' differs, so the stroke will be swum in a different manner. This is known as an individual's '*style*'. Remember that there are radically different ways in which to swim Breaststroke. There are however specific aspects of performance which are categorically wrong, especially since the laws of Breaststroke are so specific.

Listed below are the more common faults but the list is by no means exhaustive. When trying to remedy a fault, it is important to identify its cause by carrying out a stroke analysis (*see* pages 8–9). Once the cause is identified, select a simple practice and appropriate teaching point to help the individual achieve the desired technique.

Body Position

- Not keeping the shoulders and/or the hips level.
- Being too flat.
- Turning the head to one side.
- Moving the head excessively.
- Having one shoulder in front of the other.

Leg Action

- Not turning one or both feet.
- Not kicking to full extension.
- Failing to recover the feet up to the bottom.
- Kicking the feet at different speeds.
- Pointing one knee down and the other out.
- Not plantarflexing the feet at the end of the kick.
- Breaking the surface on the kick-back.

Arm Action

- Not keeping the fingers together and palms relatively flat.
- Moving one arm faster than the other.
- Pulling past the shoulders.
- Dropping the elbows down during the pull.
- Failing to tuck the elbows in after the pull.
- Extending the hands forwards too far apart.
- Failing to bend the arms during the pull.

Breathing and Co-ordination

- Holding the breath.
- Kicking and pulling all at the same time.

Laws of the Sport

Please note that it is not necessary to know the numbers of the laws. These are referred to only for reference to their inclusion in the ASA publication, *The Laws of the Sport*. They are edited to include only the information required for the ASA Assistant Teacher (Swimming) course. Further information on the laws concerning Starts, Turns and Finishes would be given on a teacher course. It is important to remember that knowledge of the laws is not only necessary for competitive purposes, but also in relation to many ASA awards.

Breaststroke

513.2 From the beginning of the first arm-stroke after the start, and after each turn, the body shall be kept on the breast. It is not permitted to roll on to the back at any time.

513.3 All movements of the arms shall be simultaneous and in the same horizontal plane without alternating movement.

513.4 The hands shall be pushed forwards together from the breast, on, under or over the water. The elbows shall be under the water except for the final stroke at the finish. The hands shall be brought back on or under the surface of the water. The hands shall not be brought back beyond the hip line, except during the first stroke after the start and each turn.

513.5 All movements of the legs shall be simultaneous and in the same horizontal plane, without alternating movement.

513.6 The feet must be turned outwards during the propulsive part of the kick; a scissors, flutter or downward dolphin kick is not permitted. Breaking the surface of the water with the feet is allowed unless followed by a downward dolphin kick.

513.8 During each complete cycle of one arm-stroke and one leg-kick, in that order, some part of the swimmer's head shall break the surface of the water.

Chapter 10
Butterfly

Butterfly Technique
General Points

- Butterfly is the second-fastest stroke.
- It evolved into a competitive stroke (from Breaststroke) in the early 1950s.
- Compared to other strokes, Butterfly demands greater upper body strength as well as more flexibility, particularly of the spine.
- Butterfly is not used extensively in competitive swimming training due to the demands it places on strength; and also because of the risk of injury to swimmers from the wide-flinging recovery of the arms.

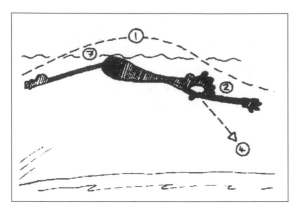

Fig. 10.1 *Butterfly body position (a)*

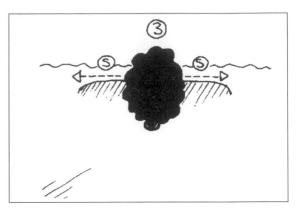

Fig. 10.3 *Butterfly body position (c)*

Body Position

ESSENTIAL POINTS

The overall position of the body changes throughout one complete cycle of the arms.

1 The body will undulate (be 'wave-like').

2 The top of the head faces forwards, which helps the swimmer recover the arms more easily and keep the hips high.

3 The head should be kept still, except when breathing. It should also be positioned centrally.

4 The eyes look forwards and downwards. The face looks downwards.

5 The shoulders should be parallel to the surface of the water, whether above or below (*see* ASA Law 514.2, page 114).

6 The shoulders should be kept square to the direction of travel.

7 The hips should be kept in line with the shoulders and as high in the water as possible, to maximise streamlining.

8 The legs should also be kept in line with the hips and shoulders, again for maximum streamlining.

Fig. 10.2 *Butterfly body position (b)*

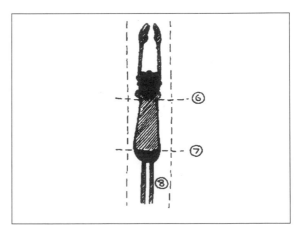

Fig. 10.4 *Butterfly body position (d)*

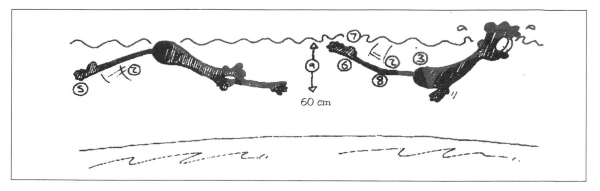

Fig. 10.5 *Butterfly leg action (a)*

Leg Action

The major function of the leg-kick is to help keep the hips as high as possible in the water. The second downkick of the complete cycle of one arm action will also help to provide propulsion, although this will vary among swimmers depending on the size of the kick. More buoyant swimmers, or swimmers who maintain a low position over the water when recovering the arms, may be able to minimise the size of the kick and conserve more energy for the arm action. Generally, however, the performance of an efficient kick is essential for a good stroke.

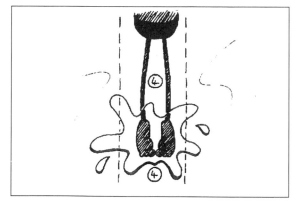

Fig. 10.6 *Butterfly leg action (b)*

ESSENTIAL POINTS

1 The legs kick simultaneously (*see* ASA Law 514.4, page 114).

2 The kick is continuous when the normal two kicks per arm cycle are performed.

3 The kick should be initiated in the powerful hip muscles.

4 The legs should be close together, although slightly apart at the knees, to allow the feet to intoe.

5 The feet should be stretched away from the knee, toes pointed (plantarflexed).

6 The ankles should be loose and flexible.

7 The soles of the feet should reach the surface of the water on the upward kick, but it is not necessary for them to break it.

8 A bend in the knee will be required in order to produce some propulsion on the downward kick. The bend in the knee may actually be quite large, but should not be emphasised. The impression should be of a stretched leg.

9 The depth of kick will vary depending on the swimmer's size. The kick should however stop descending when full extension of the legs is reached; this would generally be in the range of 45–60 cm from the surface of the water.

Arm Action

Almost all the propulsion derived in Butterfly is generated by the hugely powerful arm action. It is a highly efficient action that requires upper body strength and relaxation, particularly in the recovery phase. It is a simultaneous (*see* ASA Law 514.3, page 114) continuous and accelerating action.

ESSENTIAL POINTS

Entry

1 It should be as 'clean' as possible.

2 The hands enter in a similar fashion to Front Crawl – i.e., fingertips first with the thumb-side down (or more likely thumb first). The angle in relation to the surface of the water is likely to be greater than that of Front Crawl, and could be anything up to 90 degrees.

3 The fingers should be almost together with a fairly flat palm.

4 Entry should be at a comfortable stretch, approximately level with the shoulder line. The elbow should be slightly higher than the hand on entry.

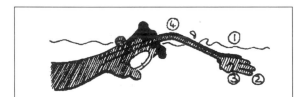

Fig. 10.7 *Butterfly arm action – entry (a)*

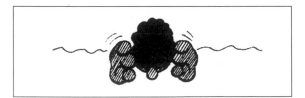

Fig. 10.8 *Butterfly arm action – entry (b)*

Propulsive phase

During the whole propulsive phase, the palm will usually face in whichever direction the hand is travelling, in addition to always facing predominantly backwards. The pathway of the hands resembles a 'keyhole' shape.

'Out and down' sweeps

1 After entry, without pause, the hands sweep outwards and downwards in an 'arc-like' shape to gain a feeling of pressure on the palm (*catch*).

2 The elbows bend progressively.

3 The elbows remain in a high position throughout, to maximise good leverage.

4 This arc should be kept relatively narrow in order to maximise streamlining and leverage.

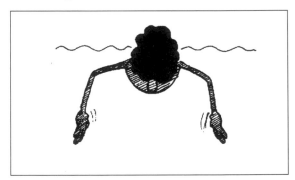

Fig. 10.9 *Butterfly arm action – 'out and down' sweep*

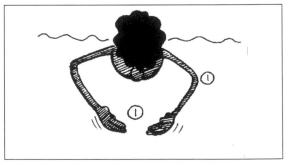

Fig. 10.10 *Butterfly arm action – insweep*

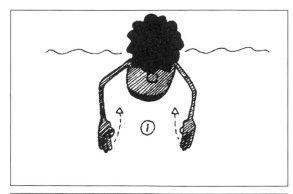

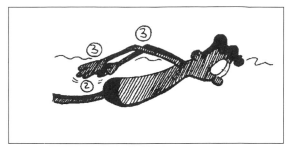

Fig. 10.13 *Butterfly arm action – recovery (a)*

Fig. 10.14 *Butterfly arm action – recovery (b)*

Figs. 10.11 and 10.12 *Butterfly arm action – the 'up and out' sweeps*

Insweep

1 The hands now sweep inwards in order almost to meet by the time they are level with the shoulders. Elbow bend will be at its maximum, approximately 90 degrees.

'Up and out' sweeps

1 The hands sweep out and up towards the surface, close by the thighs. The arms will extend gradually throughout and will reach full extension as the hands reach the thighs.

Recovery phase

1 The recovery must be over the water (*see* ASA Law 514.3, page 114).

2 Before leaving the water, the palms will rotate towards the thigh to allow for a 'clean' exit.

3 The elbows leave the water first, closely followed by the hand, little finger side up.

4 The arms are 'flung' in a low position over the water with the arms relaxed and nearly straight.

Breathing Technique

ESSENTIAL POINTS

The timing of the breathing technique with the arm action is as follows.

1a As the arms are sweeping up and out …

1b … the legs are kicking down.

1c The body will begin to rise and this is the optimum time for inhalation.

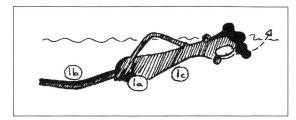

Fig. 10.15 *Butterfly breathing technique (a)*

Fig. 10.16 *Butterfly breathing technique (b)*

Fig. 10.17 *Butterfly breathing technique (c)*

2 The chin is pushed forwards and remains just in the water while inhalation takes place at the end of the push and start of recovery.

3 The face is returned to the water as the arms come approximately level with the shoulders during recovery.

4 Explosive breathing is usually used, where the breath is held and then forcibly exhaled as the mouth surfaces. However, as with the other three prone strokes, the swimmer may combine 'trickle' and 'explosive' methods. An inhalation normally takes place every second arm cycle.

Co-ordination

ESSENTIAL POINTS

The first kick-down is slightly after entry, and the second kick-down is during the upsweep.

Butterfly Practices

To follow is a list of suggested part-practices for the progressive teaching of Butterfly. This list will give you sufficient ideas for an ASA Assistant Teacher course (*see* also Chapter 12 for 'drills' for the competitive swimmer). It is by no means an exhaustive list, so if you already have ideas or practices which are not included, please try them. However, bear in mind the following.

*   Butterfly can be taught in a crude form even to beginners. Non-swimmers can perform something resembling a fly-kick.
*   However, Butterfly is more tiring than the other strokes when an over-the-water recovery is used. Practices should therefore generally be short, if using full stroke. Only the very able should do longer distances and this should be minimised to prevent the risk of injury.
*   Always optimise the chances of success.

Use the whole-part-whole approach and when teaching the part elements, generally teach in the following order: body position, leg action, arm action, breathing technique, co-ordination. Always bear in mind that it is not necessary for each element to be 'perfect' before progressing to the next – though swimmers will need to demonstrate a degree of consistency and solidarity in performance. Remember also that a few elements may be interdependent – for example, kicking powerfully will keep the hips up in order to maintain a good body position.

You may not be able to swim butterfly because you were never taught it. Don't let the children in your care become non-fly swimmers just because you don't teach it. *Teach it regularly!*

Body Position

STATIC PRACTICES

1 While standing in shallow water, shoulders under, submerge the face to *crown* level (rather than the more commonly taught brow level in the other strokes) (Fig. 10.18).

2 Holding the rail, submerge the face until the crown of the head is in, at the same time extending the arms and legs (Fig. 10.19).

Fig. 10.18 *Butterfly body position – static practices (a)*

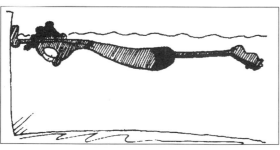

Fig. 10.19 *Butterfly body position – static practices (b)*

Fig. 10.20 *Butterfly body position – static practices (c)*

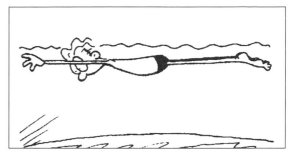

Fig. 10.21 *Butterfly body position – static practices (d)*

3 Floating in shallow water, prone and extended with the head in at crown level while holding floats (Fig. 10.20), progressing to practice (4) .

4 As practice (3) above, but without floats (Fig. 10.21).

MOVING PRACTICES

Quite often, floats can be an inhibiting factor when a swimmer is trying to achieve a correct body position – particularly when the leg action is added later. Therefore, try where possible to encourage practise without floats.

Fig. 10.22 *Butterfly body position – moving practices (a)*

1   Stand a few paces from the wall, shoulders submerged, arms extended. Push and glide with the head in at crown level. Increase the distance until a kick would be required to reach the wall (Fig. 10.22).

2   Stand with the back to the wall, shoulders submerged. One foot pushes against the wall to glide. Emphasise extension, level shoulders and waterline at the crown (Fig. 10.23).

3   Hold the rail, both feet against the wall – shoulders in, head in, hands slide under to a stretch. Then push until the whole body is stretched (Fig. 10.24). (Same emphasis as in practice (2) above.)

4   'Dolphin dives'. Stand in shallow water, with the shoulders submerged, arms extended. 'Spring' forwards and slightly upwards while submerging the head and flexing the spine to appear like a dolphin surfacing and submerging (Fig. 10.25).

Fig. 10.23 *Butterfly body position – moving practices (b)*

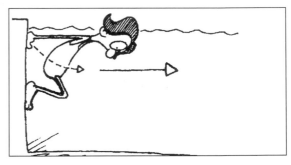

Fig. 10.24 *Butterfly body position – moving practices (c)*

Fig. 10.25 *Butterfly body position – moving practices (d)*

Leg Action

STATIC PRACTICES

1 Sitting on the pool edge, kick feet simultaneously to make a small splash (Fig. 10.26).

2 Overgrasping the gutter, with extended arms and head in to crown level, kick for varying lengths of time without inducing stress (Fig. 10.27). As with the other strokes, rail practices have limited value because the swimmer does not experience movement and so will not receive any internal feedback. There is also a small risk of injury if repeated too often and for too long.

Fig. 10.26 *Butterfly leg action – static practices (a)*

Fig. 10.27 *Butterfly leg action – static practices (b)*

MOVING PRACTICES

1 As Fig. 10.20, but starting from the rail and adding the kick (Fig. 10.28). (Remember that some may find the practice more difficult with floats.)

2 As Fig. 10.23, but adding kick and gradually increasing the distance (Fig. 10.29).

3 Progress to body position moving practice (3) (Fig. 10.24), add kick, gradually increasing the distance (Fig. 10.30).

Fig. 10.28 *Butterfly leg action – moving practices (a)*

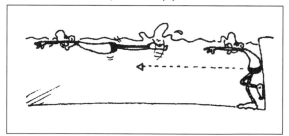

Fig. 10.29 *Butterfly leg action – moving practices (b)*

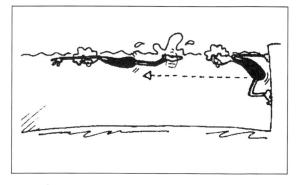

Fig. 10.30 *Butterfly leg action – moving practices (c)*

Fig. 10.31 *Butterfly leg action – moving practices (d)*

4 Lying in a supine position, gently push off into a stretched position and add the kick, gradually increasing the distance (Fig. 10.31).

5 As in practice (4) above, but 'throwing' the arms over the water until they are extended beyond the head. Add kick and gradually increase the distance (Fig. 10.32).

Developing strength in the leg action
These practices should be used once the kick is accurate. Both can also be performed with the arms extended beyond the head.

1 Push and glide under the water and perform the kick with arms kept by the side (like a 'frogman') (Fig. 10.33). Ensure that the swimmer does not push too deep and that they are aware of the wall at the other side of the pool.

2 Push and glide under the water in the supine position (Fig. 10.34). Perform the kick with the same considerations as in practice (1) above.

Fig. 10.33 *Developing strength in the Butterfly leg action (a)*

3 Push and glide from a prone position and rotate to the side, positioning the highest hand on the thigh. Add kick. Remember to swap sides (Fig. 10.35).

4 Push and glide, kick in a prone position and use a float in a vertical position to provide additional resistance (Fig. 10.36). (Some swimmers may find this difficult to perform due to the undulating nature of the body.)

Fig. 10.34 *Developing strength in the Butterfly leg action (b)*

Fig. 10.32 *Butterfly leg action – moving practices (e)*

Fig. 10.35 *Developing strength in the Butterfly leg action (c)*

Fig. 10.36 *Developing strength in the Butterfly leg action (d)*

Arm Action

STATIC PRACTICES

1 Standing in shallow water, shoulders submerged and head in at crown level, practise the arm action (Fig 10.37). (As with the other prone strokes, if the swimmer is efficient in doing this, they should feel forward movement. There-

Fig. 10.37 *Butterfly arm action*

fore, the duration of the practice should be kept to a minimum since they will be receiving no internal feedback.)

MOVING PRACTICES

1 As practice (1) above, but walking across the width (Fig. 10.37).

2 Push glide and add the kick. Perform an elongated Breaststroke arm action and recover the hands under the body. Gradually increase the distance (Fig. 10.38).

3 As practice (2) above, but adding one over-the-water recovery, approximately half-way across the width. Gradually increase the number of over-the-water recoveries (Fig. 10.39 on p. 112).

Fig. 10.38 *Butterfly arm action – moving practices (a)*

Fig. 10.39 *Butterfly arm action – moving practices (b)*

Breathing Technique

STATIC PRACTICES

1 Stand in shallow water, shoulders sub-merged, head in at crown level. Practise pushing the chin forwards to lift the mouth just clear of the water to inhale (Fig. 10.40).

2 As in practice (1) above, adding the arm action to co-ordinate the arms and breathing (emphasise blowing out hard as the mouth is just surfacing) (Fig. 10.41).

MOVING PRACTICES

1 Walk, practising the arm action and breathing every second stroke (Fig. 10.42).

2 As Fig. 10.39, breathing initially once per width, as the arms are recovered over the water. Gradually increase the number of breaths until a breath every second arm cycle is achieved. (Some swimmers may want to breathe every arm cycle.)

Fig. 10.40 *Butterfly breathing technique – static practices (a)*

Fig. 10.41 *Butterfly breathing technique – static practices (b)*

Fig. 10.42 *Butterfly breathing technique – moving practice*

Butterfly Teaching Points

Remember that each time the swimmer performs a practice, they should be given a point of technique to think about (the *teaching point*). Each point should be positive, relevant to the lesson aim and as stimulating as possible. You should endeavour to expand your repertoire of points as much as possible; this will greatly enhance your teaching success. Below is a sample of the more common Butterfly teaching points, both formal and more imaginative.

Body Position

- Keep your head still and in the middle.
- Make the top of your head go first.
- Pretend you are a wave on the ocean.
- Pretend you are a dolphin swimming by a big ship.
- Keep your shoulders level with each other.
- Make yourself a straight line.
- Be 'cool', keep yourself loose.

Leg Action

- Kick your legs at the same time as each other.
- Pretend you are a mermaid – or merman – and you have a big tail.
- Kick your legs all the time.
- Make your ankles loose.
- Kick powerfully from your bum or tummy.
- Stretch your toes away from you.
- Keep your legs quite close together.

Arm Action

- Make both arms work simultaneously.
- Put your hands in the water, in line with your shoulders.
- Make your thumbs go in first.
- Keep your fingers together and palms nearly flat.
- Make your hands trace the shape of a keyhole under the water.
- Keep your elbows high under the water and bend gradually as you pull.
- Push your hands all the way back to your thighs.
- Speed up your hands as you pull.
- Make your arms go wide and low over the water.
- Pretend you are an albatross.

Breathing and Co-ordination

- Push your chin forwards to breathe every two armpulls.
- Put your face back in as your arms come over the water.
- Blow out hard as your chin comes up.
- Kick hard as your hands go in and again as your hands go under your tummy.

Butterfly Faults

Each person's interpretation of 'the desired Butterfly technique' will differ, so that they will swim the stroke in different ways. This is known as an individual's '*style*'. There are however specific aspects of performance which are categorically wrong, especially since the laws of Butterfly are so specific. Listed below are the more common faults, but the list is by no means exhaustive.

Generally speaking, when trying to remedy a fault, it is important to identify its cause by carrying out a stroke analysis (*see* pages 8–9). Once the cause is identified, select a simple practice and appropriate teaching point to help the individual achieve the desired technique. Bear in mind that as Butterfly is taught less than the other strokes (incorrectly so!), it is quite possible that the swimmer is not performing the stroke correctly solely due to inexperience.

Body Position

- Not keeping the shoulders and/or the hips level.
- Leading with the brow of the head instead of the crown.
- Remaining too stiff in the spine, limiting undulation too much.
- Having one shoulder in advance of the other.

Leg Action

- Not kicking the legs simultaneously.
- Failing to kick up to the surface.
- Kicking from the knee.
- Having the legs too wide apart.
- Keeping the ankles too stiff.

Arm Action

- Failing to clear the water with the arms.
- Having the fingers too far apart and/or the hands cupped.
- Not pulling all the way back to the thighs.
- Pulling with the arms too straight.
- Not following the pathway of something like a keyhole.

Breathing and Co-ordination

- Holding the breath.
- Lifting the head too much to breathe.
- Pausing the arms on entry.
- Only kicking once per arm cycle.

Laws of the Sport

Please note that it is not necessary to know the numbers of the laws. These are referred to only for reference to their inclusion in the ASA publication, *The Laws of the Sport*. They are edited to include only the information required for the ASA Assistant Teacher (Swimming) course. Further information on the laws concerning Starts, Turns and Finishes would be given on a teacher course. It is important to remember that knowledge of the laws is not only necessary for competitive purposes, but also in relation to many ASA awards.

Butterfly

514.2 The body shall be kept on the breast and both shoulders shall be in line with the normal water surface. Underwater kicking on the side is allowed. It is not permitted to roll on to the back at any time.

514.3 Both arms must be brought forwards together over the water and brought backwards simultaneously.

514.4 All movements of the feet must be executed in a simultaneous manner. Simultaneous up-and down movements of the legs and feet in the vertical plane are permitted. The legs and feet need not be at the same level but no alternating movements are permitted.

Additional Skills

Chapter 11
Survival Skills

There are numerous skills which can be considered to promote survival. These would be taught to swimmers of the same ability range that you will encounter on an ASA Assistant Teacher course. The skills are normally taught in the contrasting activity section of an orthodox lesson, for an appropriate length of time – usually around five minutes. Occasionally, a whole lesson may take place which revolves around a range of survival skills. The lesson could consist of any of the following skills.

- Swimming a distance, and/or in clothes.
- Climbing out of the pool.
- Safe entries (jumping in, sliding in, straddle jumps, tuck jumps, shallow dives).
- Heat preservation techniques (HELP and Huddle positions).
- Floating.

Some of these skills will be covered in other aspects of the course: such as Health and Safety, and water confidence. However, according to ASA regulations (*see* Table 1.1, page 3), there are three specific survival skills for which you must have both technical knowledge and teaching experience:

- treading water (Breaststroke, 'egg-beater', cycling and flutter);
- surface diving (head- and feet-first);
- sculling (head-first, feet-first and stationary).

Treading Water

The skill of treading water aids survival principally by keeping the head clear of the water's surface. This prolongs survival time and delays the onset of hypothermia. It also has other applications, in other aquatic fields:

- life saving
- water polo
- synchronised swimming
- aquafit.

There are a number of different ways to tread water, any of which are acceptable. Whichever method of kicking is preferred, the arm action and body position remain constant.

Fig. 11.1 *Treading water – body position*

Body Position
ESSENTIAL POINTS

1 Keep the head above the surface of the water.

2 Remain as vertical and as stationary as possible. This may be amended to a slightly prone position if any forward movement is needed.

3 Keep the shoulders beneath the surface.

Fig. 11.2 *Treading water – arm action (a)*

Fig. 11.3 *Treading water – arm action (b)*

Fig. 11.4 *Treading water – Breaststroke kick*

Arm Action

ESSENTIAL POINTS

1 Move the hands, following the pathway of a figure-of-eight on its side.

2 As the hands sweep on their outward path, they are pitched at an approximate angle of 45 degrees with the little finger uppermost.

3 As the hands sweep on their inward path, they are pitched at an approximate angle of 45 degrees with the thumb uppermost.

4 The action is continuous.

5 The hands are almost flat, with the fingers together or almost together.

6 The action remains beneath the surface.

7 The arms bend at the elbow to approximately 90 degrees.

Leg Action

ESSENTIAL POINTS

Breaststroke kick
1 Feet turned out and upwards towards the shin (dorsiflexed).

2 Legs kick simultaneously.

3 Feet kick out and down towards the pool floor, with a wide action to increase surface area and so assist floatation.

4 Pressure should be smooth and constant to minimise the 'bobbing effect' associated with this method of treading water.

Egg-beater kick
1 Similar to Breaststroke kick above, but alternating instead of simultaneous kicking.

Fig. 11.5 *Treading water – Egg-beater kick*

Fig. 11.6 *Treading water – Cycling kick*

Cycling kick

1 Soles of the feet press down towards the pool floor.

2 Maintain a high degree of knee-bend.

3 Alternate between a steady and an exaggerated bike-riding position (as if you were in 27th gear!).

Flutter kick

1 Feet are plantarflexed.

2 Wide action.

3 Extended legs as in Front Crawl, but in a vertical position.

Teaching Treading Water

Since the skill of treading water is performed in deep water, it is essential that you are sure the swimmer is confident and relatively proficient before practising it. This does not mean to say that there isn't much you can achieve in respect of this skill, *before* they become a more proficient swimmer.

ARM ACTION

1 Swimmers stand in water just covering the shoulders and practise the arm action while copying your demonstration (Fig. 11.8).

2 Wearing a rubber ring, armbands or arm-discs, practise the arm action fairly close by the poolside but in deep water (Fig. 11.9).

Fig. 11.8 *Teaching the arm action (a)*

Fig. 11.7 *Treading water – Flutter kick*

Fig. 11.9 *Teaching the arm action (b)*

Fig. 11.10 *Teaching the arm action (c)*

Fig. 11.11 *Teaching the leg action (a)*

3 Holding the pool edge or gutter with one hand, practise the arm action with the other hand while simultaneously practising the leg action. Remember to swap sides (Fig. 11.10).

4 As in practice (3) above, but using a float for support instead of the pool edge (Fig. 11.10).

LEG ACTION

Just as when the swimmer was learning to swim, give them the opportunity to find the stroke that best suits them (this is known as the *multi-stroke* method). You should also let the swimmers explore the kick which best enables them to tread water with success. You could let them try the four varieties of kick with all the following practices, until their clear favourite is established.

1 Sitting on the pool edge, kick the legs in as near-vertical position as possible (Fig. 11.11).

2 Holding the pool rail, kick in a vertical position (Fig. 11.12).

3 Wearing buoyancy aids, kick in a vertical position (Fig. 11.13).

Fig. 11.12 *Teaching the leg action (b)*

Fig. 11.13 *Teaching the leg action (c)*

Fig. 11.14 *Teaching the leg action (d)*

4   Use a float under each arm (Fig. 11.14).

5   Use only one float under one arm, then swap arms (Fig. 11.15).

6   Finally, practise the whole skill using the preferred kick, initially close by the poolside (Fig. 11.16).

Developing strength in the leg-kick

These practices should be used once the kick is fairly accurate and a clear head position is maintained with little or no stress. It may now be a good idea to also practise the kick or kicks with which they have less success.

1   Kick but use only one hand to scull (simulating an injury to the other arm) (Fig. 11.17).

Fig. 11.15 *Teaching the leg action (e)*

Fig. 11.16 *Teaching the leg action (f)*

Fig. 11.17 *Developing strength in the leg-kick (a)*

Fig. 11.18 *Developing strength in the leg-kick (b)*

Fig. 11.19 *Developing strength in the leg-kick (c)*

Fig. 11.20 *Developing strength in the leg-kick (d)*

Fig. 11.22 *Developing strength in the leg-kick (f)*

3 Kick, signalling with one hand to raise assistance in a survival situation (Fig. 11.19)

4 Kick, signalling with both hands to raise assistance in a survival situation (Fig. 11.20).

5 Kick while holding a brick. This could be held above the surface for varying lengths of time (Fig. 11.21).

6 Challenge swimmers to tread water for a specified length of time (beware of the boredom factor) (Fig. 11.22).

7 You can use treading water for many other activities, as it liberates swimmers to be 'free' of the poolside without support. For example, teach a group of children how to pass and receive a ball in water polo. Have fun! (Fig. 11.23)

2 Kick using no arm action (simulating the possible need to immobilise the other limb) (Fig. 11.18).

Fig. 11.21 *Developing strength in the leg-kick (e)*

Fig. 11.23 *Treading water can be fun!*

Fig. 11.24 *The head-first surface dive – approach*

Fig. 11.26 *The head-first surface dive – the dive (b)*

Surface Diving

The skill of surface diving aids survival by enabling the swimmer to submerge safely and be able to swim under an 'obstacle' of some description. It also has other applications, in other aquatic fields:

- life saving
- synchronised swimming
- octopush.

There are two different methods of surface diving: head-first, or feet-first. Both of these are acceptable if they provide the swimmer with the opportunity to submerge safely. There are circumstances in which one might be preferable to the other – these will be discussed on page 128. Both methods can be broken down into the following phases:

- approach
- the dive
- transition to swim
- surfacing.

Head-first Surface Dive

ESSENTIAL POINTS

Approach

1 Breaststroke is normally used, although in a survival situation it would be foolish for a swimmer who is more proficient in Front Crawl to use anything different.

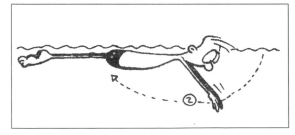

Fig. 11.25 *The head-first surface dive – the dive (a)*

Fig. 11.27 *The head-first surface dive – the dive (c)*

2 The swimmer should calm themselves as they approach the point of diving and ensure that they breathe normally.

The dive

1 The chin is tucked into the chest.

2 The hands sweep in a Breaststroke-type action, from a position in front of the swimmer downwards and backwards to the thighs.

3 The head and upper body are thrust downwards.

4 The body pikes (bends) at the waist.

5 The legs begin to lift simultaneously and together, towards a vertical position out of the water.

6 Air may be gently exhaled to assist the descent.

7 The hands change to sweep back and downwards towards the bottom of the pool.

8 The arms are kept together in a straight line in advance of the head until the feet are submerged.

Transition to swim

1 The chin may be lifted forwards to enable a more horizontal swimming position to be achieved.

2 The hands move from an extended position to either a Breaststroke-type action or a paddling action.

3 The eyes are kept open and focus directly in front.

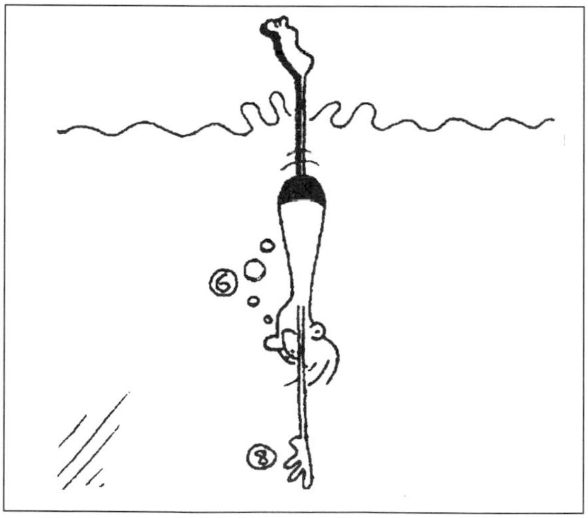

Fig. 11.28 *The head-first surface dive – the dive (d)*

Fig. 11.29 *The head-first surface dive – transition to swim*

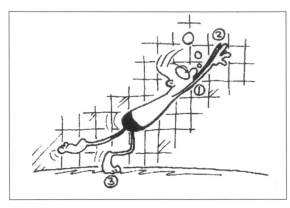

Fig. 11.30 *The head-first surface dive – surfacing (a)*

Surfacing

1   The chin is lifted upwards to initiate the surface.

2   The arms are moved to a position in advance of the head for protection.

3   Either a push from the floor, or a kick to reach the surface.

4   As the hands break the surface, the arms are 'flung' sideways to rest on the surface and prevent re-submersion.

Fig. 11.31 *The head-first surface dive – surfacing (b)*

Teaching Surface Diving

When teaching surface diving, it is essential to be aware of the depth of water that the practice is being performed in. Care should always be taken to ensure that there is no risk of the swimmer injuring their head in collision with the pool floor. It is also necessary to be aware of the risk to the internal ear if repeated practice takes place in deep water.

Approach

1   Swim Breaststroke to a given point with head out, and then submerge the face (Fig. 11.32).

The dive

1   Stand in shallow water and practise submerging the head and gently exhaling (Fig. 11.33).

2   Start with the arms extended in front. Pull the hands back to the hips while submerging the head and piking at the waist (Fig. 11.34).

3   Do handstands in shallow water (Fig. 11.35.

4   Swim into a handstand (Fig. 11.36).

Fig. 11.32 *Teaching surface diving – approach*

Fig. 11.33 *Teaching surface diving – the dive (a)*

Fig. 11.34 *Teaching surface diving – the dive (b)*

Fig. 11.35 *Teaching surface diving – the dive (c)*

Fig. 11.36 *Teaching surface diving – the dive (d)*

Transition to swim

1 From a handstand position, lift the chin forwards to swim 'on the pool floor' (Fig. 11.37).

2 From a handstand position, swim forwards to pass through a submerged hoop (Fig. 11.38).

3 Experiment with different methods of swimming underwater (Fig. 11.39).

Fig. 11.37 *Teaching surface diving – transition to swim (a)*

Fig. 11.38 *Teaching surface diving – transition to swim (b)*

Fig. 11.39 *Teaching surface diving – transition to swim (c)*

Fig. 11.40 *Teaching surface diving – surfacing (a)*

Fig. 11.42 *The feet-first surface dive – approach (a)*

Fig. 11.43 *The feet-first surface dive – approach (b)*

Fig. 11.41 *Teaching surface diving – surfacing (b)*

Surfacing

1 From a sitting position on the pool floor in the shallow end, extend the arms above the head and push to surface (Fig. 11.40).

2 Stand in shoulder-deep water, arms beneath the surface. Lift the arms up to full stretch above the head and then 'slap' arms down on to the surface (Fig. 11.41).

Feet-first Surface Dive

This method of surface diving is much safer when water conditions are unknown – i.e., when water clarity is poor or there are underwater hazards, such as rocks.

ESSENTIAL POINTS
Approach

1 Either Breaststroke or Front Crawl to a stationary position just prior to the point of the 'obstacle'. Tread water by swimmer's chosen method (Figs 11.42 and 11.43).

The dive

1 The legs kick downwards powerfully (usually Breaststroke action), as the hands press down slightly to raise as much of the body above the surface of the water as possible (Fig. 11.44).

2 The arms are immediately thrown above the head into a vertical position to ensure that the maximum possible amount of the body is out of the water. This will now initiate rapid submersion (Fig. 11.45).

3 The whole body should be kept vertical and streamlined from the fingertips to the toes, until the fingertips have submerged (Fig. 11.46).

Fig. 11.44 *The feet-first surface dive – the dive (a)*

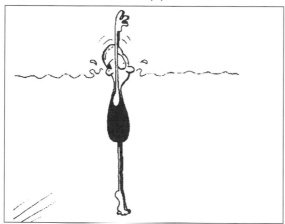

Fig. 11.45 *The feet-first surface dive – the dive (b)*

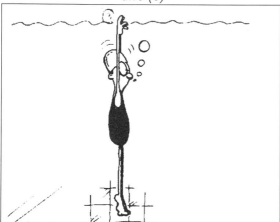

Fig. 11.46 *The feet-first surface dive – the dive (c)*

Transition to swim

1 The hands are drawn down from an extended position to close to the chest (Fig. 11.47). (They may also press upwards towards the surface to assist with further submersion.)

2 The chin is pulled down towards the chest as the shoulders descend, and the body bends at the waist to achieve a horizontal position (Fig. 11.47).

3 The hands move forwards to an extended position, to either a Breaststroke-type of action or paddling type of action (Fig. 11.48).

4 The eyes focus on a point directly in front of the swimmer (Fig. 11.48).

Surfacing

The points are the same as for a head-first surface dive *see* page 126.

Fig. 11.47 *The feet-first surface dive – transition to swim (a)*

Fig. 11.48 *The feet-first surface dive – transition to swim (b)*

Teaching the Feet-first Surface Dive

Approach

1 Swim to a given point and rotate from horizontal to achieve a vertical, 'treading water' position (Fig. 11.49).

The dive

1 Stand in shallow water. Jump up to sit on the pool floor (Fig. 11.50).

2 Stand in shallow water with arms above the head. Bend knees to 'slide ' beneath the surface (Fig. 11.51).

3 As in practice (2) above, but jump up to slide down (Fig. 11.52).

4 Swim in deeper water. Stop to tread water; 'fling' the arms upwards to descend until the toes touch the pool floor and then push to surface (Fig. 11.53).

Fig. 11.49 *Teaching the feet-first surface dive – approach*

Fig. 11.51 *Teaching the feet-first surface dive – the dive (b)*

Fig. 11.50 *Teaching the feet-first surface dive – the dive (a)*

Fig. 11.52 *Teaching the feet-first surface dive – the dive (c)*

Fig. 11.53 *Teaching the feet-first surface dive – the dive (d)*

Fig. 11.54 *Teaching the feet-first surface dive – transition to swim (a)*

Fig. 11.55 *Teaching the feet-first surface dive – transition to swim (b)*

Transition to swim

1 As Fig. 11.53, but as the feet touch the floor, bend the knees, and descend the head and shoulders to swim forwards (Fig. 11.54).

2 As in practice (1) above, but swimming forwards through a submerged hoop (Fig. 11.55). (This could be started initially in shallower water, and then progress to deeper water.)

Surfacing

The practices are the same as for the head-first surface dive – *see* page 128.

Sculling

The skill of sculling aids survival purposes by enabling the swimmer to propel themselves over weeds without risk of entanglement. It also allows the swimmer to propel themselves, even if they have sustained a leg injury. Sculling has other applications, in other aquatic fields:

• synchronised swimming
• water polo
• swimming strokes.

There are numerous methods of sculling in the field of synchronised swimming. In a survival context, there are three main methods:

• head-first
• feet-first
• stationary.

Whichever method is used, the body position is the same.

Fig. 11.56 *Sculling body position*

Body Position

ESSENTIAL POINTS

1 The head is still, ears just submerged, eyes looking upwards.

2 The whole body – including the legs – is as near horizontal as the individual's body type will allow. The whole position should be as close to the surface as possible.

3 The feet should be plantarflexed.

Arm Action

ESSENTIAL POINTS

There are a few common points of technique, irrespective of the method being performed.

1 The action is continuous just below the surface – approximately level with the buttocks.

2 The pathway follows that of a figure-of-eight lying on its side.

3 The action takes place close by the side of the body with relatively straight arms.

4 The fingers are kept either together or almost together, and the palms are almost flat.

5 On the outward sweep, the little finger is uppermost. On the inward sweep, the thumb is uppermost.

6 The action is contained within approximately a body's width either side of the swimmer.

To change the direction of travel, all that is necessary is to change the pitch of the hands while ensuring that all the above points are being performed.

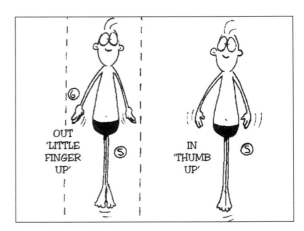

Fig. 11.58 *Sculling arm action (b)*

Fig. 11.57 *Sculling arm action (a)*

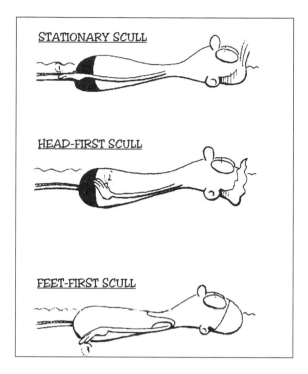

Fig. 11.59 *Stationary sculling*

Stationary Scull

ESSENTIAL POINTS
The fingertips point directly in a line parallel with the water's surface.

Head-first Scull

ESSENTIAL POINTS
The fingertips are pitched upwards so that an angle of 45 degrees between the forearm and back of the hand is formed.

Feet-first Scull

ESSENTIAL POINTS
The fingertips are pitched downwards towards the pool floor so that an angle of 45 degrees between the forearm and palm of the hand is formed.

Teaching Sculling

Practices will be the same, irrespective of the direction that is required.

BODY POSITION
All static Back Crawl body position practices are appropriate – *see* pages 79–80.

ARM ACTION
1 Standing in shoulder-deep water, practise the arm action (Fig. 11.60).

2 Wearing a rubber ring or other buoyancy aids, practise the arm action (Fig. 11.61).

Fig. 11.60 *Teaching sculling – arm action (a)*

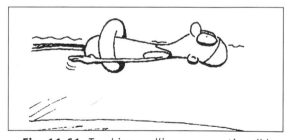

Fig. 11.61 *Teaching sculling – arm action (b)*

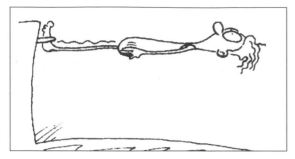

Fig. 11.62 *Teaching sculling – arm action (c)*

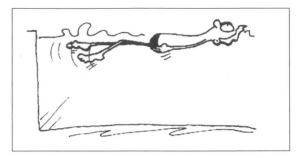

Fig. 11.65 *Teaching sculling – arm action (f)*

3 If a rail is available, hook the feet under it and practise the arm action (Fig. 11.62).

4 Holding the gutter with one hand and lying in a supine position adjacent to the wall, practise with the other hand. Remember to swap sides (Fig. 11.63).

Fig. 11.63 *Teaching sculling – arm action (d)*

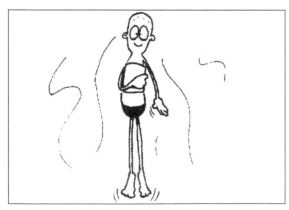

Fig. 11.64 *Teaching sculling – arm action (e)*

5 Holding a float across the chest, practise with the other hand. Remember to swap sides (Fig. 11.64).

6 Push and glide (supine). Kick to maintain a floating position and practise arm action (Fig. 11.65).

Developing strength in the arm action

These practices are used once all three actions are accurate and a horizontal, stable body position is maintained.

1 Challenge the swimmer to perform a set distance in a fast time, or to complete a greater distance (Fig. 11.66).

2 In a vertical position, scull without kicking and raise the body to chest level out of the water for varying lengths of time (Fig. 11.67).

3 In a horizontal position, carry a brick resting on the stomach (Fig. 11.68). (Ensure there is no risk of the brick falling off and injuring anyone.)

4 In a horizontal position, tow someone by hooking the feet under the armpits. (The partner should make no propulsive movements.) This practice is only possible while performing a head-first scull (Fig. 11.69).

Fig. 11.66 *Developing strength in the sculling arm action (a)*

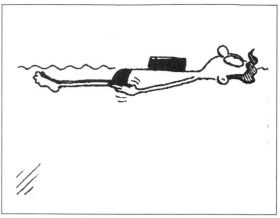

Fig. 11.68 *Developing strength in the sculling arm action (c)*

Fig. 11.67 *Developing strength in the sculling arm action (b)*

Fig. 11.69 *Developing strength in the sculling arm action (d)*

Chapter 12
The Club Swimmer and Environment

During an ASA Assistant Teacher course, you will spend approximately one third of your practical teaching time with more able swimmers. Some of this time will be in a club-type training set-up. This immediately brings into play practical aspects which have not been covered elsewhere in the book.

Lane Swimming

The swimmers will usually swim lengths rather than widths. The pool will therefore normally be roped off in lengths, although on occasion you may also experience a set-up which is a mixture of both lengths and widths.

Most pools used for club swimming are 25 metres long. There are however a number of other different sizes, as follows: 20 yards, 20 metres, 25 yards, 33⅓ yards, 36⅔ yards, 33⅓ metres, and – very occasionally – 50 metres. Most pools have four, six or eight lanes. The size of the pool, and number of lanes and swimmers, will dictate the work which the coach has set.

It is essential that extreme safety is exercised when sorting out the direction of travel. Quite simply, the swimmers in one lane must travel in the opposite direction to swimmers in the adjacent lane, while swimming in chain formation – i.e., clockwise or anti-clockwise. This will minimise the risk of collision of arms, or of arms and heads, during over-the-water recovery movements.

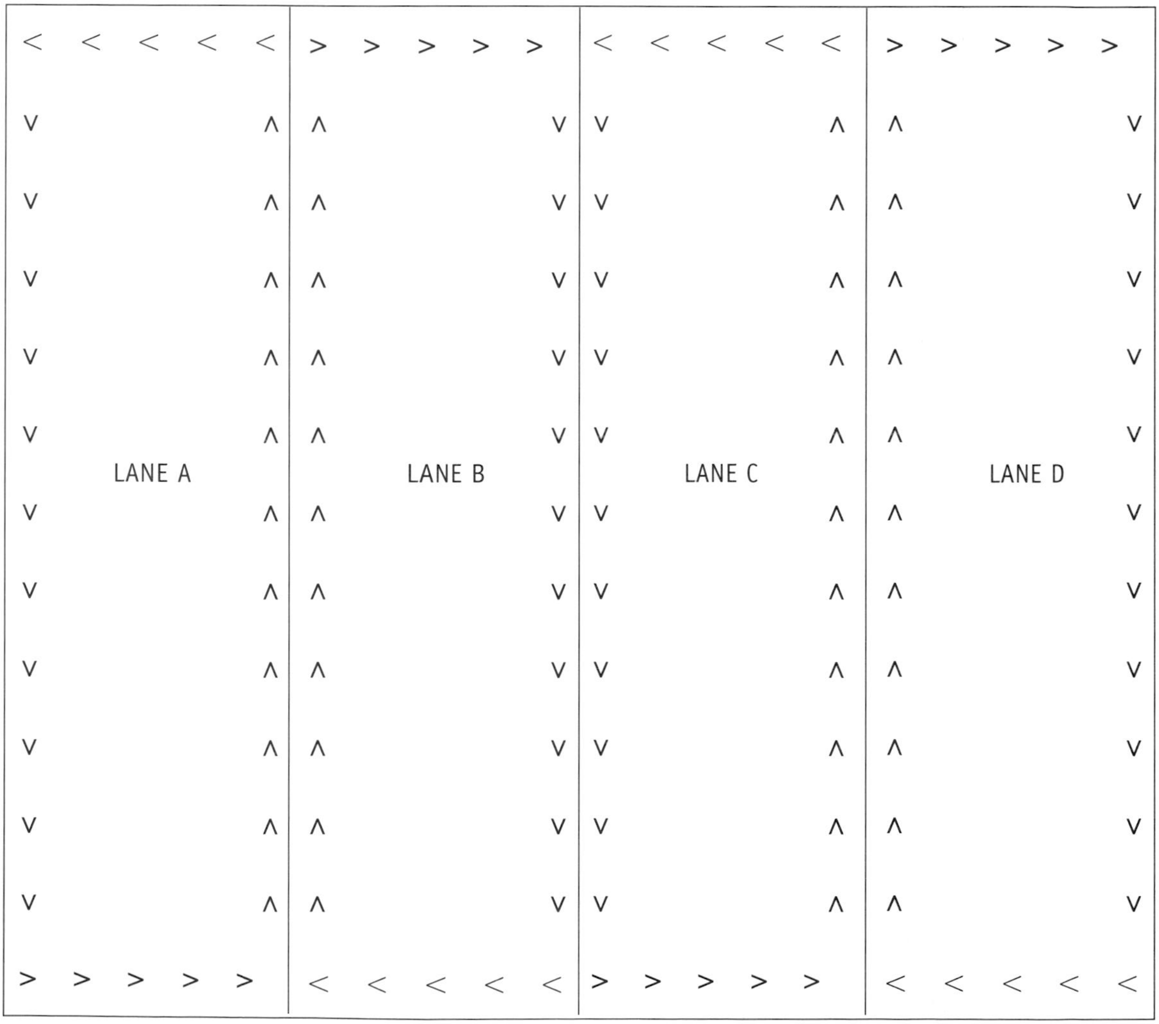

Fig. 12. 1 *Direction of travel when lane swimming*

Many clubs would also organise the lanes, for example, with the most able swimmers in lane A and the next most able in lane B, etc. It is essential that swimmers are grouped in a lane according to their ability. This will ensure that from a safety point of view, they will not catch up other individuals. To this end you would also organise the swimmers so that the fastest leads off the lane and the rest set off in rank order; however, remember that this may change depending on the stroke or distance being swum. (A swimmer may be the fastest at Front Crawl and yet the slowest at Breaststroke.)

It is not always necessary to swim in a chain formation. On occasion, depending on the content and focus of the session, the swimmers may swim lengths in a wave formation. For example, lanes A, B and C may be swimming in a chain, while lane D swims lengths and climbs out to walk back. It would still be necessary to ensure that the swimmers remain on the appropriate side of the lane for safety, even when swimming in waves, if other lanes are swimming in a chain.

Another safety consideration is the amount of time that elapses between the swimmers setting off. This is usually five seconds, although on odd occasions it may be three or ten seconds. This would depend on the work being carried out and the number of swimmers in the lane.

The Teacher/Coach

After a swimmer has experienced a degree of solid, considerate teaching and practising in a 'teaching' environment, the best way to progress is to move to length swimming and to establish and expand speed and endurance in a 'coaching' environment. The role of teacher and coach are similar, with the major difference being that the teacher's primary concern is the development of the swimmer's technique and confidence, while the coach focuses on the more physiological aspects. It must be stressed that both roles cross over. The teacher will undoubtedly from time to time work on stamina and speed, while the coach will focus on accuracy of performance and confidence in racing.

Teachers or coaches will often decide early in their careers which type of swimmer they would prefer to deal with on an ongoing basis – although others will work with all ability levels. You may not have a choice, it may be decided for you. It is however exceptionally important to be able to deal with swimmers of all abilities and be empathetic to the role of all teachers and coaches, irrespective of the swimmers that they work with.

The Swimmer

The swimmers that you will experience in the club environment will be about seven or eight years old and upwards. They should have a reasonable degree of proficiency so as to be able to swim for a longer period of time without deterioration of technique.

Whatever the level of swimmer, it is essential that they are not placed under undue stress, especially the younger swimmers. (There will be odd occasions when the coach might expose the older swimmers to the stress of competition, while still in a training environment.)

Session Work

Since the majority of work carried out in this type of environment is principally aimed at developing the physiological systems of the swimmer, you should normally be working from a 'training schedule' written for you by the course tutor or coach. On occasion, however, you may write a session which is designed more to develop technique or to develop stamina in the less able club swimmers, applying the basic principles of work and rest.

When devising a session or schedule which is aimed at a more advanced swimmer, with the principle focus being physiological, there are four main factors to consider:

- *D*istance
- *I*nterval
- *R*epetitions
- *T*ime.

If at any time the technique of the individual's performance deteriorates, then you should examine carefully the content to see if it is too stressful.

DISTANCE

The distances used in a training schedule vary, although the most commonly used are 50 metres, 100 metres and 200 metres. There are two reasons why these are advantageous:

- they usually comprise an even number of lengths, and so management is made easy – the swimmer always ends the swim at the same end of the pool, eradicating the need for a clock at both ends and the need for you to move around excessively;
- they are also the distances swum most often in competition.

INTERVAL

This is the amount of rest taken at the end of each swim. It may be as little as five seconds or as much as two minutes, depending entirely on the focus of the work in any session and more specifically in any part (*set*) within it. The most common amount of rest given varies between fifteen and thirty seconds.

REPETITIONS

This may be defined as the number of times that a swim is repeated. Occasionally, a set may also be repeated.

TIME

This is the amount of time that the swim will take. Again it will vary depending on the focus of the work. It may be as short as twenty seconds or as long as thirty minutes.

The Training Schedule (Session)

This will be split into sub-sections just like a normal teaching plan. The sections have a slightly different emphasis. You will find an example in your log book, section 3, page 5. You should also be working from a schedule supplied by your course tutor or coach. The sections are as follows:

- warm-up
- main theme (*set*)
- sub-theme (*set*)
- swim-down (*cool-down*).

WARM-UP

This is used to ensure that the swimmer is thoroughly 'loose' and that all muscles are warm and ready for intense activity without the risk of injury.

MAIN THEME

The bulk of the work takes place in this section. It could be endurance, speed or technique work, depending on the time of the year and the particular part of the coach's cycle (*scheme of work*).

SUB-THEME

If the main theme has been largely aerobic work (endurance), then this section may be based on speed or technique, for example.

SWIM-DOWN

This is a critical part of any session, often neglected through lack of time. It allows the swimmer's bodily functions to come to rest gradually, instead of abruptly. It also helps the swimmer to relax and gives time for the body to disperse waste products which have built up in the muscles during exercise – thus helping to prevent injury and speed up the readiness for exercise again in the shortest possible time.

Evaluation and Record-keeping

After any training schedule – just as with any type of 'lesson' – you should carry out an evaluation as outlined in Chapter 3 (*see* pages 30–32). In addition, you should record the times of swimmers for particular parts of the session (the different sets). An example might be:

Ethel – 1st set (10x50 m free off 15 sec r.i.) 45,45,45,45,46,47,47,48,50,50

This would be most helpful in future planning, as the above figures clearly indicate that Ethel was either tiring as the set progressed, or that she was unable to pace herself and thus set off too fast. You might be able to offer the following advice: 'Your target time for each repetition is 47 seconds.'

In order for you to record times, it will be most beneficial if you have the use of a stopwatch. There are numerous types which have the facility to time ten or more laps and to recall times. This would undoubtedly make your task easier.

The following is an example of how to time swimmers in a lane.

- Start the watch as swimmer (1) sets off (the rest of the swimmers will usually be setting off at five-second intervals, using the clock or your command on the watch. If there are few enough swimmers in the lane and the resting period allows, ten-second intervals will make your job easier).
- As swimmer (1) finishes, push the lap button on the stopwatch (usually the top left). As each subsequent swimmer finishes, push the same button. After all swimmers have finished, recall the times.
- The first time is straightforward, as this is the complete time for swimmer (1). For swimmer (2), subtract five seconds from the second recall time; for swimmer (3), subtract ten seconds from the third recall time, and so on.

You must remember that, if using a set where the rest is only fifteen seconds, the swimmers may need you to set them off again by your command if no clock is available. This may prevent you from timing all swimmers, or timing every repetition.

Being able to use a stopwatch is very important. Practise as much as possible.

Examples of Session Goals

- To improve **endurance** (aerobic capacity).
- To improve **speed** (anaerobic capacity).
- To improve **technique** of …

These are basic examples; a coach may choose different, more specific aims. On an ASA

Assistant Teacher course, you should not have to work out what a swimmer should do to improve anything other than their technique. The examples which follow are to give you an idea of how the coach will decide an appropriate set of work for a specific aim.

TO IMPROVE ENDURANCE

This type of aim will usually involve more work than rest. An example might be:

- 10 x 50 metres Front Crawl with 15 seconds R.I.;
- 10 **R**epetitions of 50 metres **D**istance with an **I**nterval of rest of 15 seconds. If it took the swimmer 45 seconds to complete the swim (**T**ime) then the work to rest ratio would be 3:1. (This is a common ratio for aerobic work.)

Aerobic work is usually carried out at 70–80 per cent intensity. You can measure this by two methods. For example, if you wanted a swimmer to work at an intensity of 80 per cent, you would do the following.

- Take the swimmer's personal best time for the distance being performed at that stroke, for example, 75 seconds for 100 metres Front Crawl.
- Add 20 per cent of the time (i.e. 15 seconds), to give the required time at 80 per cent effort. While this is not strictly mathematically accurate, it is the method which coaches usually use.
- The target time for the swimmer to work at 80 per cent effort is 90 seconds; this is then the work period (**T**ime).
- If using a ratio of 3:1, the rest period would be 30 seconds (i.e., 90 divided by 3).
- The total time in which the swim should be completed – including the rest – is now 120 seconds; this is commonly referred to as the 'turn-around time' or 'off 2 minutes (120 seconds)'. You may

see this written as: 10 x 100 metres Front Crawl off 2 minutes.

An alternative method of working a swimmer at a given intensity is to work from their pulse rate. Once again, if you were working at an intensity of 80 per cent, the example would be as follows.

- The maximum pulse rate is 220.
- Take from this the swimmer's age – for example, 20.
- The individual's maximum pulse rate is 200.
- Now *subtract* 20 per cent (i.e. 40) to give the target pulse rate (160 after each swim).
- As the swimmer finishes the swim, check the pulse in the neck (carotid pulse) for 6 seconds (a tenth of a minute) and add a zero to the result to give the beats per minute.
- This gives a fairly accurate pulse rate, enabling you to discern whether the swimmer is working either too hard, or too easily. 15(0) would be working slightly too easily; 17(0) would be working slightly too hard.

TO IMPROVE SPEED

This type of aim will usually involve equal rest and work – or more rest than work. An example might be:

- 6 x 100 metres Front Crawl off 2 minutes 45 seconds (165 seconds)

To improve speed, the intensity of effort needs to be 90 per cent plus. Use the same swimmer as an example – i.e., personal best time of 75 seconds:

- add 10 per cent, i.e., 7.5 seconds; the target time is 82.5 seconds (for 90 per cent effort);
- using the turn-around time of 165 seconds, this individual would be working

at a work to rest ratio of 1:1, since the work and rest are equal (82.5 seconds);

- Alternatively, using the pulse rate, 200 (maximum) minus 10 per cent (20)— target pulse is 180.

It is a good idea to get used to the simple arithmetic which is necessary to calculate these methods of working, to give you a better understanding of what the coach is aiming for. Try these examples. The answers can be found at the end of the chapter.

- Calculate an 80 per cent effort swim of an individual whose best time is 65 seconds.
- Calculate the pulse rate required for a swimmer who is 15 years old to swim at an intensity of 90 per cent.
- Calculate the turn-around time for a swimmer to work at a ratio of 3:1 work to rest, when their target time is 60 seconds.

There are many different types of 'set', used to achieve different goals. It would not be appropriate to list them here, as this would be more appropriate to Teacher Certificate level. Whenever you assist a coach, ask them to explain any sets you are unsure of; you will soon become familiar with the systems used.

Most sessions involve a high degree of work at an aerobic intensity designed to increase the swimmer's endurance. However, this will not help greatly in competition and so it is essential that the swimmer trains fairly regularly without too much stress at a higher intensity. This would be decided by the coach. A great deal of work in a session is done using Front Crawl, since it is the least injurious stroke to both the swimmer and other individuals in their own and other lanes.

TO IMPROVE TECHNIQUE

There is always room for improvement in the stroke technique of most swimmers. 'Tinkering' for the sake of it should however be avoided. In a 'coaching environment', it will be necessary to teach techniques which the swimmer has probably not yet experienced in a 'teaching environment' – for example, how to do a Back Crawl turn using the flags suspended five metres from each end of the pool as a guide. This skill is not part of an ASA Assistant Teacher course.

It is not a good idea to attempt to improve technique when a swimmer is tired during a session, or if you would interfere with another physiological aim of the session by talking to them when they should in fact be working. A coach would not be happy if you attempted to change someone's stroke when they had a competition approaching in the near future.

At the end of this chapter, you will find a list of drills (practices) which may be used in a training session to improve both technique and strength.

Equipment

You will undoubtedly encounter some equipment that is not used in a teaching environment.

The Pace Clock

This is often placed at the shallow end of the pool, since a great deal of swims start and end here. The swimmers need the clock to time the 'gap' between them setting off, the time it took them to complete the swim, and when to swim again. You may need to do this for them in the early stages.

- The gap is usually five seconds, or on occasion ten seconds – and rarely, three seconds.

- The time that it took to complete the swim is the difference between the time they set off and the time they finished.
- The time to swim again is after a given rest, or on the 'turn-around time'.
- O'clock is often referred to as the 'top', while half-past is often called the 'bottom'.

Backstroke Turn Flags

These are suspended five metres from either end of the pool to indicate to the swimmer that the end of the pool is near. With practice, the swimmer will be able to work out how many more strokes are required and so eliminate the need to turn around to look.

Pool Floor Markings

The black lines painted on the pool floor indicate the centre of a lane. The 'T' at the end of the black line indicates two metres from the end of the pool. Both assist the swimmer in gauging when to start a tumble turn in Front Crawl, or when to spot the turn or finish in Breaststroke and Butterfly.

Goggles

Use of these should be encouraged so as to minimise the risk of collision. Their *safe* use should be emphasised; ensure they are not pulled away from the face.

Kickboards

These are oversized floats. Most are of a conventional shape, although some more recent designs are more radical – often with in-built handles and a provision for the face to be submerged, thus promoting a more natural body position and hence less injury to backs and shoulders. Whichever design is used, kickboards facilitate the practice of kicking sets or drills.

Flippers

These are worn as an extension to the feet and increase the surface area, allowing the swimmer to swim faster than normal and so having to work harder. Most are of the conventional shape which have been worn for many years, although again, there are now more radical designs available (often called 'zoomers' or 'force fins'). These allow the swimmer to swim faster but without the speed of the leg action being slowed which normally happens with conventional fins. Irrespective of the design used, flippers facilitate the practice of kicking sets or drills.

Pull-buoys

These are as used in the teaching context, although once again, more streamlined shapes have been introduced recently. All are used in pulling sets (where arms only are used), or arm drills.

Hand or Finger Paddles

These are large pieces of plastic which are fitted to the palm. They increase the size of the hand and so allow more power to be generated; the swimmer is thus able to swim faster than normal. The use of paddles requires more strength, and so has a good training effect. Over-use should be avoided to prevent injury. Paddles are used in pulling sets or during arm drills.

Drag-belts

These are usually worn around the waist, although some are worn around the feet. They are made of a series of little 'cups', or of foam, and work either by filling up with or absorbing water, thus slowing the swimmer and resulting in more effort being required. The same effect can be achieved by wearing a T-shirt, although this may slightly inhibit arm movement. The variety of drag-belt that fits around the waist can be used during any set or drill. Over-use of this type of aid should be avoided to minimise the risk of injury through overworking.

Sports Bottles

Depending on the nature of the work, it may be necessary for swimmers to replace fluids during a session. Excessive use of these should be discouraged.

Drills

The following are a selection of commonly used drills (practices) for club swimmers.

Front Crawl

KICKING
Almost all practices are performed using a kickboard. Variations include the use of fins and the possibility of kicking beneath the surface.

ARM DRILLS
'**Catch up**' From a position of both arms extended, one arm completes a full cycle, (propulsion–recovery–entry). As soon as it has done so, the other arm completes a full cycle, and so on.

'**Chicken wing**' There are two variations of this drill. The first of these should only be used for very short distances and very sporadically. Swim with the thumbs in armpits and elbows high. Swim Front Crawl. As the arm recovers, keep the elbow high and brush the thumb past the ear.

'**Fist swimming**' Swim with the hands in a fist. (There are also other examples where the swimmer may swim with fingers wide open, or curled, etc.)

Back Crawl

KICKING
These are often performed *without* the use of a kickboard. Variations again include the use of fins and possibly kicking beneath the surface of the water, sometimes using a fly-kick.

ARM DRILLS
Single-arm drills Stroking for given distances, using one arm only.

'**Catch up**' The same as in Front Crawl above.

'**Rope swimming**' Pulling on the lane ropes, usually up one side of the lane and down the other side.

Butterfly

KICKING
These are often performed *without* the use of a kickboard. Again, they may be performed both with fins and beneath the surface.

ARM DRILLS
Single-arm drills Stroking for given distances using one arm only.

Combining single and normal pulling Both arms extended, right arm pulls, recovers then enters. Left arm then does the same, followed by both arms (a normal fly-arm pull).

Breaststroke

KICKING

Most drills are performed using a kickboard. The drills are largely the same as those detailed in Chapter 9, particularly those for developing leg strength.

ARM DRILLS

Static drill Lying with the chest resting on a lane rope, practise the arm action with an emphasis on keeping the action in front of the shoulders.

Moving drills Most are performed with the use of a pull-buoy or a fly-type kick.

Single-arm drill Leave one arm outstretched and perform a single-arm action with the other arm. This may be repeated a given number of times, or be followed by the other arm immediately.

Co-ordination drills Perform Breaststroke in the following order – kick, kick, pull.

All the drills are offered as examples of the kind of practice which club swimmers are expected to perform. It is important to stress that some of these can be detrimental to the stroke if performed over too long a period of time. All the practices detailed in the stroke chapters can be adapted to club swimmers, particularly those aimed at developing leg strength.

ANSWERS TO THE QUESTIONS ON PAGE 142

- *Calculate an 80 per cent effort swim of an individual whose best time is 65 seconds.*
  Answer – 78 seconds. The mathematically correct answer is 81.30 seconds, calculated in the following way – 100 divided by 65 = 1.54 metres per second. 80 per cent of this is 1.23 metres per second. 100 metres at 1.23 metres per second is 81.30 seconds. This may explain why the more simple, if slightly incorrect, method highlighted on page 142 is used.

- *Calculate the pulse rate required for a swimmer who is 15 years old, to swim at an intensity of 90 per cent.*
  Answer – 185 (rounded up).

- *Calculate the turn-around time for a swimmer to work at a ratio of 3:1 work to rest, when their target time is 60 seconds.*
  Answer – 1 minute 20 seconds.

Glossary

arm-disc A disc of polystyrene or other such material, fitted around the upper arm to provide buoyancy.

cannon swimming A teaching method where one swimmer sets off on a given signal or point, followed by subsequent swimmers as they reach the same point or signal.

dorsiflexed Turning the toes up towards the kneecap.

drag-belt A device fitted around the waist of a swimmer to provide resistance.

drogue effect Where a baggy costume acts as an anchor.

EAP The Emergency Action Plan.

eddy currents The turbulence behind the swimmer which slows them down.

feedback Information given to the pupil – either verbally or visually – about their performance.

fins Worn as an extension of the feet to provide more power.

kickboard The large float used for the practice of kicking.

multi-stroke method The teaching technique used where pupils have the opportunity to experience and learn the strokes with an equal emphasis and where non-swimmers are able to pursue the stroke with which they have the most success (while not neglecting the others).

non-swimmer For the purposes of this book, a pupil who still relies on fitted buoyancy aids in order to propel themselves.

NOP The Normal Operating Procedure.

pace clock The clock situated at the end of the pool with a very large second hand.

plantarflexed Pointing the toes away from the kneecap.

practice The task set for the swimmer 'to do'.

profile resistance The resistance to forward motion made by the shaping of the body.

progressive part-practice The method whereby the practices gradually become more demanding as the lesson progresses.

pull-buoy The floatation device used between the thighs.

rubber ring An inflatable device worn around the chest to provide a high degree of buoyancy.

swimmer For the purposes of this book, a pupil who can propel themselves completely unaided.

teaching point The point of technique for the swimmer to 'think about' as they perform the practice (task).

Teflon A substance used to coat some costumes to reduce viscosity.

viscosity The 'stickiness' of a fluid.

wave swimming Splitting swimmers using numbers (1, 2, 3) or names (Boyzone, Spice Girls, Fish, Chips, etc.). The first wave sets off, followed by the next wave as they receive a signal or reach a given point.

whole-part-whole method The swimmer practises the strokes in this order during a whole lesson, to enhance their chances of attaining the skill. They will start and finish with a whole-stroke practice which will be interspersed with progressive part-practices; and further whole-stroke practices.

Recommended Reading

There are many other publications which you may find useful. The ASA Awards Centre at 1, Kingfisher Enterprise Park, 50 Arthur Street, Redditch, Worcs. B98 8LG has an extensive publications list. Telephone 0800 220292.

Particularly recommended are the following.

An Introduction to Swimming Teaching and Coaching by F. Dalrymple-Smith, J. Lawton and V. Way (1995)

The Competent Swimmer by A. Eakin (1993)

Swimming Games and Activities by A. Cregeen and J. Noble (1999)

I hope that this book has proved useful in helping you achieve the necessary criteria, and that you are now in a position to go on to the 'next rung of the ladder' – The ASA Teacher Certificate (Swimming). If you do intend to progress, it will be essential for you to order a copy of the *Teacher Certificate Log Book* from the above address, and to purchase a copy of the publication *Swimming Teaching & Coaching Level 1* – again, available from the above address.

Good Luck!

Index